A Vegan Taste of France

Other cookery books by Linda Majzlik published by Jon Carpenter

A VEGAN
TASTE *of* FRANCE

Linda Majzlik

Jon Carpenter

Our books may be ordered from bookshops or (post free) from
Jon Carpenter Publishing, Alder House, Market Street, Charlbury,
England OX7 3PH

Please send for our free catalogue

Credit card orders should be phoned or faxed to 01689 870437
or 01608 811969

First published in 2003 by
Jon Carpenter Publishing
Alder House, Market Street, Charlbury, Oxfordshire OX7 3PH
☎ 01608 811969

© Linda Majzlik 2003

Illustrations by Amanda Henriques © 2003

The right of Linda Majzlik to be identified as author of this work has been
asserted in accordance with the Copyright, Designs and Patents Act 1988

ISBN 1 897766 82 3

Printed in England by J. W. Arrowsmith Ltd., Bristol

CONTENTS

Accompaniments

Sauces and dressings

Breads

Baking

INTRODUCTION

France is the third largest country in Europe and in terms of agricultural output it is the most important. From the cooler, moist conditions in the north to the warmer Mediterranean climate in the south, the country is well suited to growing a variety of crops and it is self-sufficient in the production of basic foods. As well as supplying the home market, French produce such as cereals, nuts, fruits, vegetables, mustard, brandy and wines are a familiar sight in the many countries to where they are exported. Because of the diverse growing conditions in France, the cuisine is notably regional and each area has its own culinary traditions and specialities, based around the local produce. Examples of some of these specialities are the multitude of apple dishes and cider-flavoured casseroles from Normandy where orchards dominate the countryside, the buckwheat pancakes and breads of Brittany where buckwheat is a major crop, and ratatouille and olive-based dishes from the south where Mediterranean-type vegetables grow in the warmer climate.

Shopping for food can be a great pleasure in France. Everyday items are generally bought from small specialist food shops with their beautifully displayed wares, rather than from the super- or hypermarket, while fresh fruit and vegetables tend to be got from the local market. French shoppers demand the highest quality produce, often rejecting any item that is less than perfect. The markets in France are legendary and in Paris alone there are reputed to be at least seventy food markets. As well as these, Rungis, on the outskirts of Paris, is home to one of the largest food markets in the world. Even the smallest towns have at least a few stalls where shoppers can buy local produce.

The French take considerable pride in their culinary skills and meals are prepared with great care and attention to detail. Many classic dishes can be traced back for generations and some of these have become favourites around the world. The main meal was traditionally eaten in the middle of the day, but many families now prefer to wait until the evening so that the whole family can eat together. Whenever it is eaten, the main meal is a lengthy affair consisting of three or four courses and often accompanied by plenty of locally-produced wine. Other meals tend to be much lighter, with only one or two courses.

As well as the usual public holidays, several religious feast days are celebrated throughout the year, and on these days families and friends often gather together and prepare special foods which are served as part of the celebrations.

France is famous for the great variety and number of its cafés, bistros and restaurants and eating out is a favourite pastime for many French people.

It may be hard to believe, but from the time of the ancient Gauls until the end of the 19th century the basic diet of many French people consisted mainly of cereals, beans, nuts and vegetables. The number of vegetarians in France is gradually increasing now, but it is still very difficult to find vegetarian meals in restaurants and veganism is almost unheard of. However, by using the ever-growing range of animal-free alternatives to meat and dairy products it is possible for vegans to create and enjoy an authentic taste of French cuisine.

Bon appetit!

THE VEGAN FRENCH STORECUPBOARD

French cooks shop regularly in the market for the freshest seasonal fruits and vegetables and combine these with basics from the storecupboard to produce their distinctively flavoured dishes, many of which have become favourites around the world.

Almonds Grown in the south of France, almonds are regularly used in a whole host of baking and dessert recipes and occasionally in savoury dishes. They are rich in protein, vitamins and calcium and their flavour is enhanced if they are lightly toasted before use.

Apricots These are grown in central and southern areas of France and are a rich source of protein, vitamins and calcium. Dried apricots are occasionally added to casserole dishes and are also used extensively in sweet recipes, where they are often combined with almonds. Choose plump, unsulphured varieties for the best flavour.

Arrowroot A fine white starch milled from a type of root, which is used to thicken sweet and savoury sauces and jellies. It loses its thickening properties if cooked for too long.

Barley Whole or pot barley is more nutritious than pearl as it has not been stripped of essential nutrients in the milling process. An excellent ingredient in stews and casseroles and also served cooked as an accompaniment.

Beans Haricot beans are an essential ingredient in cassoulet - a rich, hearty casserole which originated in the south of France. Other popular beans include borlotti, flageolet and red kidney and these are used in a variety of cooked dishes and salads. All beans are a good source of protein, fibre and minerals. They can be cooked in bulk, divided into portions and frozen successfully.

Breadcrumbs Essential for gratin toppings and croustades and as an ingredient in various other savoury and sweet recipes. Breadcrumbs can easily be made by whizzing bread in a food processor or nut mill until crumbled. They can be stored in the freezer and used from frozen.

Buckwheat flour Milled from the triangular grain, buckwheat flour is greyish in colour and gluten free. It is especially popular in Brittany, where it is used to make savoury pancakes. Buckwheat flour is also mixed with other flours for bread.

Capers These small green flower buds from a trailing Mediterranean bush have a piquant taste and are sold preserved in either vinegar or brine. They are used as an ingredient and also as a garnish.

'Cheese' A very good range of vegan substitutes made from soya are available from health food shops and some supermarkets. They can be used in various recipes, from sauces to gratin toppings, or simply grated and sprinkled on cooked dishes as a garnish.

Chestnuts As well as being a favourite ingredient in French cuisine, chestnuts grown in France are exported to many other countries. Cooked chestnuts have a soft, floury texture. Chestnuts preserved in sugar syrup are known as marrons glacés and are served as a dessert. Both fresh and dried chestnuts are used in various pâtés, stews and casseroles or mixed with cabbage as an accompaniment. Dried chestnuts need to be soaked in boiling water for an hour, then simmered for about 45 minutes until tender.

Chickpeas Creamy, nutty-flavoured chickpeas make a good addition to soups and stews and are also served cold in salads. Like beans they are highly nutritious and also freeze well.

Cornflour A very fine starchy white flour which is milled from corn. It is sometimes known as cornstarch and is used to thicken sauces.

'Cream' Soya cream is an excellent alternative and can be used to make ice creams or simply spooned over desserts as a topping.

'Cream cheese' An excellent vegan alternative made from soya is available from health food shops.

Dijon mustard A mixture of ground mustard seeds and spices, Dijon mustard has quite a mild flavour and is reputedly the most popular variety in

France. As well as simply being served as a condiment it is also an essential
culinary ingredient.

Dried mushrooms Highly regarded for their rich, intense flavour, dried
mushrooms need to be reconstituting in warm water before use. Although
expensive, they are only used in small quantities so a little goes a long way.

Garlic Indispensable in the French kitchen, garlic is not only valued for its
flavour but also for its medicinal properties. Loose bulbs or strings of garlic
keep well for a couple of months if stored in a cool, dry place. Choose firm
bulbs made up of plump individual cloves for the best flavour. Chewing fresh
parsley after eating garlic is reputed to freshen the breath.

Gherkins A variety of small cucumber, sold pickled in jars with dill-flavoured
vinegar. They are used to add their distinctive sweet-sour flavour to tartare
sauce and salad dressings.

Hazelnut butter Available from health food shops, hazelnut butter is a richly
flavoured mixture of ground hazelnuts and oil. It can help to bind mixtures
and is also delicious spread on home-made bread.

Hazelnuts Loiret and Dordogne are the main hazelnut-producing areas in
France and the French are particularly fond of little hazelnut biscuits and
hazelnuts dipped in chocolate. They are best bought whole for grinding or
chopping at home and their flavour is greatly enhanced if lightly toasted.

Herbs Both fresh and dried herbs are used in French cuisine and these are
sold alongside vegetables in the numerous markets throughout France.

Basil The large, aromatic, scented leaves of the basil plant combine particularly well with aubergines and tomatoes. Fresh whole leaves make a flavourful
addition to green salads.

Bay leaves These dried, aromatic leaves of an evergreen tree are added to stews
and casseroles to impart their distinct, strong and slightly bitter taste. Dried
leaves have more flavour than fresh, and ground bay leaves are used sparingly
for a more concentrated flavour.

Bouquet garni Although bouquet garni mixtures can be bought in little
muslin bags, ready for adding to stews and casseroles, French cooks often
make their own by wrapping sprigs of fresh parsley, thyme, rosemary and a
bay leaf in a piece of leek. This is tied with a length of cotton and discarded
before the dish is served.

Chervil With similar leaves to parsley, chervil has a subtle, fresh flavour that combines well with other herbs. It is often used as a garnish.

Chives Used to impart a mild and subtle oniony flavour and also used as a garnish.

Dill A feathery-leafed herb with a distinctive aniseed flavour which combines well with potatoes, cabbage and carrots and also makes an attractive garnish.

Fines herbes A mixture of parsley, chervil, tarragon and chives, used fresh or dried.

Herbes de Provence A mixture of dried herbs consisting of thyme, rosemary, bay leaf and basil.

Marjoram This tiny-leafed herb has a very distinct, aromatic flavour and is often mixed with other herbs when 'mixed herbs' are called for.

Mint There are numerous varieties of mint available, but the most commonly used ones are probably peppermint and spearmint. Mint goes particularly well with peas, mangetout and potatoes and whole fresh leaves can be added to green salads.

Oregano A small-leafed herb that has a natural affinity with tomatoes and one which retains its flavour well when dried.

Parsley This universally popular herb is used liberally in savoury dishes and combines well with other herbs. Fresh parsley is also widely used for garnishing and the flat-leafed variety is favoured in France.

Rosemary The thin pine needle-type leaves of this strongly flavoured, sweet and fragrant herb are used to flavour vinegars and oils and are also combined with other herbs when 'mixed herbs' are called for.

Tarragon A typically French herb, tarragon has thin pointed leaves and a very distinctive aniseed flavour. It is particularly popular in sauces and dressings.

Thyme A highly aromatic, small-leafed herb which retains its flavour well in the drying process. It is regularly used in various savoury dishes and combines particularly well with mushrooms and tomatoes.

Jam A vast range of sugar-free jams, sweetened with fruit juice concentrate, and fruit spreads made by reducing concentrated fruit juices are now produced and these are used in various baking recipes. Once opened they need to be kept refrigerated.

Lentils The blue-green puy lentil originates in central France and is excellent for making pâtés, savoury fillings, soups and salads. Red and green lentils are also popular and all are a good source of protein, fibre, vitamins and minerals.

Linseed Also known as flaxseed, these shiny little brown seeds are a rich source of essential fatty acids. They are often combined with other seeds when making seeded breads.

Maizemeal Ground yellow maize, which is also known as cornmeal, is used to add its distinctive flavour to savoury bread recipes.

Mayonnaise Some excellent egg-free versions are available in health food stores and some supermarkets. Mayonnaise is an essential ingredient in some dressings and sauces and for rémoulade.

Olive oil An intrinsic ingredient in French cuisine, both for cooking and for making dressings. There are countless varieties to choose from, all with varying tastes. Extra virgin oil is considered to be the best and is also the most expensive.

Olives These are grown extensively in the south of France and a visit to any French market will reveal the number of varieties that are available. Olives are used as an ingredient or for garnishing or simply eaten whole or stuffed as starters. They are available preserved in either oil or brine.

Parmesan An authentic-tasting vegan version made from soya is available from health food stores and some supermarkets. It is used as a garnish and in toppings for various savoury dishes.

Pine kernels These tiny fragrant nuts with a sweet creamy taste are the seeds of a variety of pine tree. They are used in savoury toppings and also as a garnish.

Prunes Plums are a favourite fruit all over France and prunes are the dried fruit of a black-skinned variety. They are a valuable source of iron, calcium and vitamins and are used in both sweet and savoury recipes. Prunes can be bought either pitted or unpitted and the no-need-to-soak type are the most tender.

Puff pastry This can be difficult and time consuming to make, so ready-made puff pastry is used in the recipes in this book. Vegan versions are readily available from supermarkets.

Rice Red rice is a speciality of the Carmargue region in the south of France. It has a unique nutty texture and flavour and is served plainly cooked or mixed with other ingredients. Long grain rice is a popular accompaniment for stews and casseroles and is also used to make timbales and terrines.

Sesame seeds These tiny protein- and calcium-packed seeds are used in bread recipes, sprinkled on top of pastry before cooking and used in salads.

Soup mix Available ready-made, but it is equally easy to make your own by mixing equal quantities of lentils, pot barley, wheatgrain and split peas. It makes an excellent, nutritious base for vegetable soups, stews and casseroles.

Soya milk Unsweetened soya milk has been used in both sweet and savoury recipes.

Spices Although spices are not used nearly as much as herbs in French cuisine, some spices are considered essential for flavouring certain dishes.

Black pepper A universally popular seasoning for savoury dishes. Freshly ground black peppercorns are preferred.

Cayenne pepper The dried fruit of a hot red pepper. Deep red in colour and very pungent, cayenne is used to add 'heat' to a dish.

Celery seed These tiny lightish-brown seeds are occasionally used sparingly to impart an aromatic celery flavour to savoury dishes.

Cinnamon Used in its stick and ground form, cinnamon has a warm, comforting, sweet flavour and is used in various cake and dessert recipes.

Cloves These dried buds of an evergreen tree are valued for their anaesthetic and antiseptic qualities. Whole cloves are used to flavour syrups, whilst ground cloves are used, sparingly, particularly in dishes containing apples and pears.

Coriander seed With a mild, sweet, orangey flavour which is more pronounced when the seeds are lightly crushed, this spice is occasionally used to flavour cabbage dishes.

Fennel seed The dried seeds of a plant in the parsley family impart an aniseed/licorice flavour and are sometimes used in stews, especially with tomatoes.

Green peppercorns These unripened berries are softer and milder than black peppercorns. They are often used to flavour marinated olives.

Mixed spice A mixture of several ground sweet spices which is used for flavouring spiced clafoutis in particular, but is also useful for adding a spicy flavour to dried fruit compotes.

Mustard seed These seeds come in three different colours, yellow (sometimes called white), brown and black and the pungency increases with the darkness of the seeds. Their flavour is released when the seeds are crushed and mixed with liquid and they are traditionally used to flavour choucroute and marinated olives.

Onion seeds These crunchy, black, pear-shaped seeds have a pleasant mild oniony flavour and are used in particular for sprinkling on bread dough before baking.

Paprika The ground dried pod of a sweet red pepper, paprika adds colour and a mild sweet flavour to savoury dishes, especially those containing tomatoes.

Sun-dried tomatoes The unique and intense flavour of sun-dried tomatoes enriches tomato-based dishes. They are also used in savoury bread recipes and are available dry, for reconstituting in water, or preserved in olive oil, ready to use.

Sun-dried tomato paste More expensive than ordinary tomato purée but it adds a distinctive richer and more intense tomato flavour.

Sunflower seeds Rich in protein, vitamins in the B complex, vitamin E and potassium, sunflower seeds are used in seed bread recipes and as a garnish.

Textured vegetable protein A nutritious and versatile soya product which readily absorbs the flavours of the other ingredients used. Natural chunks and minced varieties are used in some savoury recipes.

Tinned tomatoes Crushed or chopped tinned plum tomatoes are used in cooked dishes to add a strong tomato flavour when fresh ripe tomatoes are unavailable.

Tomato purée Used to strengthen the flavour and add colour to tomato-based dishes.

Vegetable bouillon A vegan version is available in health food stores and makes a good alternative to home-made stock. Use a rounded dessertspoonful of bouillon per 20 fl.oz/600ml of water.

Vegetable stock Used in a whole host of savoury recipes, vegetable stock is easy to make and adds a more authentic flavour than stock cubes. It can be made in bulk and frozen in measured quantities. Peel and chop a selection of vegetables such as carrots, celery, courgette, leek, onion and potato. Put them in a large pan and add a couple of chopped garlic cloves, a few sprigs of parsley and a bay leaf. Cover with water and bring to the boil. Cover the pan and simmer for 30 minutes, then strain the liquid through a fine sieve.

Vinegar Red and white wine vinegars are favoured for dressings and for flavouring with fresh herbs. Pickling vinegar is used in making choucroute.

Wine France is renowned throughout the world for its fine wines and luckily for vegans many of these are produced without the use of animal ingredients. Wine is an essential ingredient in various soups, stews, casseroles and sauces.

Walnut oil A rich, nutty and intensely flavoured oil which is generally used in moderation because of its high cost. Walnut oil is not used for frying, but in dressings or simply drizzled over cooked vegetables to impart its distinctive taste. After opening, walnut oil should be kept in a cool dark place as it quickly becomes rancid.

Walnuts These are grown in many areas of France, with the peak production in the Rhône valley. Walnuts are believed to help lower cholesterol levels in the body and in France they are used in numerous sweet and savoury dishes or simply as a garnish. Walnut pieces are cheaper to buy than halves and are ideal for grinding and chopping.

Yeast Easy-blend dried yeast is used in the recipes requiring yeast because of its simplicity, as it does not need to be reconstituted in liquid.

STARTERS

French-style starters or hors-d'oeuvre are carefully chosen to
complement the main course and can range from simple little savoury
spreads, quickly whizzed up in a blender, to more elaborate terrines
and pâtés which can be made the day before required and refrigerated.
Slices of melon or avocado and cooked vegetables such as globe
artichokes, asparagus or courgettes, simply served with a French-style
dressing, are also typical fare. All of the following examples also make
ideal buffet foods, and some can serve as light meals when
accompanied by salads and bread.

Marinated olives

8oz/225g green olives

2 garlic cloves, crushed

1 tablespoon finely chopped lemon peel

1 bay leaf

sprigs of fresh rosemary and thyme

1 teaspoon yellow mustard seeds, lightly crushed

1 teaspoon green peppercorns, crushed

olive oil

Wash the olives and place them in a lidded jar with the garlic, lemon peel, bay leaf, fresh herbs, mustard seed and peppercorns. Cover with olive oil and put the lid on the jar. Shake the jar to distribute the flavourings and leave in a cool place for about 7 days. Drain the olives and put them in a serving bowl. The strained oil can be used for cooking or in a dressing.

Roasted red pepper dip with crudités (serves 4)

dip

1lb/450g red peppers

2 garlic cloves, chopped

2 rounded tablespoons vegan mayonnaise

1 rounded tablespoon finely chopped fresh basil

1 tablespoon olive oil

½ teaspoon paprika

black pepper

crudités

prepare a selection from the following:

mangetout and tender French beans, topped and tailed

fennel, cucumber, carrot, peppers, celery, turnip, cut into strips chicory leaves, separated

cauliflower, cut into florets

spring onions, trimmed

radishes and cherry tomatoes, halved

Put the peppers on a baking tray under a hot grill, turning occasionally, until the skins blister. Carefully remove the skins, membranes and seeds and chop the flesh. Put this in a blender with the remaining dip ingredients and blend until smooth, then transfer to a serving dish. Cover and refrigerate for a couple of hours.

Place the bowl of dip in the centre of a serving platter and surround with a selection of crudités when serving.

Green olive, caper and parsley dip (serves 4)

4oz/100g green olives, chopped

2oz/50g French bread

1oz/25g capers

1oz/25g fresh parsley, chopped

4 fl.oz/125ml water

2 garlic cloves, chopped

2 tablespoons olive oil

1 dessertspoon lemon juice

black pepper

Break the bread into pieces and soak in the water for 30 minutes. Add the remaining ingredients and blend until smooth. Spoon into a bowl and serve with crudités.

Creamy herb and garlic spread (serves 4)

6oz/175g vegan 'cream cheese'

4 rounded tablespoons finely chopped fresh mixed herbs

2 garlic cloves, crushed

black pepper

Mix the ingredients thoroughly and spread onto thin slices of bread to serve.

Tapénade (serves 4/6)

6oz/175g black olives

2oz/50g capers

2 garlic cloves

4 tablespoons olive oil

1 tablespoon lemon juice

1 teaspoon herbes de Provence

black pepper

Put all ingredients into a blender and blend until smooth. Transfer to a serving bowl and use as a spread or a dip.

Mushroom, lentil and walnut pâté (serves 6)

8oz/225g mushrooms, wiped and finely chopped

4oz/100g puy lentils

2oz/50g walnuts, grated

2oz/50g breadcrumbs

1 onion, peeled and finely chopped

2 garlic cloves, crushed

1 tablespoon olive oil

1 tablespoon red wine

½ teaspoon dried thyme

black pepper

extra olive oil

Soak the lentils in water for an hour, then drain and bring to the boil in a fresh pan of water. Cover and simmer for about 40 minutes until tender, drain again and mash. Heat the oil and gently fry the onion and garlic until soft. Add the mushrooms and fry until the juices begin to run. Remove from the heat and add the lentils, walnuts, breadcrumbs, wine and thyme. Season with black pepper and mix very well. Spoon the mixture into a 7 inch/18cm diameter greased ovenproof dish. Press down firmly and evenly and brush the top lightly with olive oil. Bake in a preheated oven at 180°C/350°F/Gas mark 4 for 30 minutes. Serve in the dish, either warm or cold, with crusty French bread.

Carrot and hazelnut pâté (serves 6)

12oz/350g carrots, scraped and chopped

4oz/100g hazelnuts, ground

2oz/50g breadcrumbs

½oz/15g soya flour

1 onion, peeled and finely chopped

1 garlic clove, crushed

4 fl.oz/125ml water

1 tablespoon olive oil

1 rounded dessertspoon hazelnut butter

1 rounded teaspoon dried chervil

pinch of cayenne pepper

black pepper

flaked hazelnuts

Fry the onion and garlic in the oil until soft, then add the carrots and water and bring to the boil. Cover and simmer until the carrots are done. Remove from the heat and strain the liquid into a small mixing bowl. Mash the carrots with a potato masher, add the ground hazelnuts, breadcrumbs, chervil and cayenne pepper and mix together well. Combine the soya flour and hazelnut butter with the strained liquid until smooth. Add this to the carrot mixture and season with black pepper. Mix thoroughly and spoon into a lined and greased 7 inch/18cm diameter flan tin. Press down firmly and evenly, then sprinkle the top with flaked hazelnuts and press these in lightly with the back of a spoon. Bake in a preheated oven at 180°C/350°F/Gas mark 4 for 30 minutes until golden. Allow to cool slightly, then keep in the fridge for a few hours until cold. Cut into wedges and serve with a salad garnish.

Aubergine and chestnut pâté pots (serves 6)

8oz/225g aubergine, finely chopped

4oz/100g dried chestnuts

1 onion, peeled and finely chopped

2 garlic cloves, crushed

2 tablespoons olive oil

1 teaspoon dried thyme

¼ teaspoon cayenne pepper

black pepper

Soak the chestnuts in boiling water for 1 hour, drain and bring to the boil in fresh water. Cover and simmer for about 40 minutes until tender, then drain again and grate the chestnuts.

Fry the aubergine, onion and garlic in the oil for 15 minutes, stirring frequently to prevent sticking. Remove from the heat and add the chestnuts and the remaining ingredients. Mix well, then divide the mixture between 6 greased 2 inch/5cm ramekin dishes, pressing it down firmly and evenly. Bake in a preheated oven at 180°C/350°F/Gas mark 4 for 35 minutes. Allow to cool, then refrigerate until cold. Serve in the dishes with crusty bread and a salad garnish.

Spinach, walnut and rice terrine (serves 6)

8oz/225g fresh spinach leaves

filling

4oz/100g long grain rice

3oz/75g walnuts, grated

3oz/75g breadcrumbs

2oz/50g mushrooms, wiped and finely chopped

1 onion, peeled and finely chopped

1 garlic clove, crushed

10 fl.oz/300ml vegetable stock

1 dessertspoon walnut or olive oil

1 teaspoon dried parsley

1 teaspoon dried thyme

black pepper

Heat the oil in a large pan and soften the onion and garlic. Add the mushrooms and fry until the juices run. Stir in the rice, stock, parsley and thyme and season with black pepper. Bring to the boil, cover and simmer gently until the liquid had been absorbed, then remove from the heat and stir in the walnuts and breadcrumbs.

Bring a large pan of water to the boil. Remove any thick stalks from the spinach, add the leaves to the boiling water and blanch for 30 seconds. Drain the leaves well and allow to cool. Line an 8 inch/20cm loaf tin with foil and grease. Use just over half the spinach leaves to line the tin, leaving an overhang to fold over the filling. Build up the layers by overlapping the leaves so that there are no gaps. Spoon half of the filling into the spinach lined tin and press down evenly. Take about half of the remaining spinach leaves and spread these over the filling to make a spinach layer. Spoon the rest of the filling on top and again press down evenly. Spread the remaining spinach over the filling and fold the overhanging leaves over to enclose. Cover with foil and bake in a preheated oven at 180°C/350°F/Gas mark 4 for 45 minutes. Allow to cool in the tin for 15 minutes, then carefully invert the terrine onto a serving plate. Cover and put in the fridge for a few hours or overnight until cold. Cut into 6 equal slices with a sharp knife.

Leek and chestnut terrine (serves 6)

1lb/450g leeks, trimmed

8oz/225g shelled fresh chestnuts

6oz/175g courgette, grated

2oz/50g long grain rice

2oz/50g breadcrumbs

1 onion, peeled and finely chopped

1 garlic clove, crushed

1 tablespoon olive oil

1 tablespoon soya flour

2 tablespoons water

1 rounded teaspoon dried chives

1 rounded teaspoon dried parsley

½ teaspoon Dijon mustard

black pepper

mixed salad leaves

fresh chervil leaves

Cook the rice until done and drain well. Put the chestnuts in a pan and cover with water. Bring to the boil, simmer for 10 minutes, then drain and grate. Fry the onion and garlic in the oil until soft. Remove from the heat and add the courgette, rice, grated chestnuts, breadcrumbs, chives and parsley. Mix the soya flour with the water and mustard until smooth and add to the mixture. Season with black pepper and combine thoroughly.

Slice the leeks lengthwise in half and separate the leaves. Put them in a large pan, cover with water and bring to the boil. Cover and simmer for 3 minutes, then drain well and allow to cool. Line an 8 inch/20cm loaf tin with foil and grease. Use three-quarters of the leeks to line the tin, leaving an overhang to fold over the filling. Build the layers up until the tin is completely lined. Spoon half of the filling into the tin, pressing it down evenly. Arrange the remaining leeks over the filling and spoon the rest of the filling on top. Press down evenly, then enclose the filling by folding over the overhanging leaves. Cover with foil and put the tin in a baking dish. Fill this three-quarters full with boiling water and place it in a preheated oven at 180°C/350°F/Gas mark 4 for 45 minutes. Leave to cool in the tin for 15 minutes, then invert onto a serving plate. Cover and refrigerate for a few hours or overnight until cold. Arrange some mixed salad leaves around the edges, garnish the top with chervil leaves and cut into thick slices.

Grilled Provence tomatoes (serves 4)

1lb/450g tomatoes, skinned and sliced

4 spring onions, trimmed and finely chopped

4 black olives, sliced

2 garlic cloves, crushed

1 dessertspoon olive oil

1 teaspoon herbes de Provence

black pepper

finely chopped fresh parsley

Arrange the tomato slices in a heatproof dish, sprinkling each layer with some of the spring onions, garlic, olives and herbs de Provence. Season with black pepper and drizzle the olive oil over the top. Place the dish under a preheated grill for about 10 minutes until the tomatoes just begin to soften. Garnish with chopped fresh parsley and serve.

Root vegetable and almond cakes (serves 4/6)

1lb/450g prepared root vegetables (e.g. potato, celeriac, carrot)

4oz/100g ground almonds

2oz/50g breadcrumbs

2 shallots, grated

1 rounded tablespoon finely chopped fresh chives

pinch of cayenne pepper

black pepper

olive oil

Cut the vegetables into even sized large chunks and put them in a pan of water, bring to the boil and simmer for 10 minutes. Drain and allow to cool, then grate the vegetables into a mixing bowl. Add the remaining ingredients apart from the olive oil, and mix thoroughly. Take rounded dessertspoonfuls of the mixture and roll into balls in the palm of the hand. Flatten each ball slightly, put them on a plate, cover and chill for a few hours. Shallow fry the cakes in hot olive oil for a few minutes on each side until golden brown. Drain on kitchen paper and serve hot with a salad garnish.

SOUPS

Soups are among the easiest and most versatile of dishes to prepare and French cooks use the freshest ingredients to make a whole range of colourful, wholesome and flavourful varieties. The French have a passion for all types of soup and usually serve light soups as an appetising prelude to the main course, while the more robust, heartier soups are served with bread and salad as a meal in themselves. Croûtons, chopped fresh herbs, 'cheese' and chopped nuts are all used as nutritious and attractive garnishes. All the following soups can be made in advance, refrigerated and simply reheated when required, or they can be frozen.

Provençal bean soup (serves 4)

8oz/225g mixed cooked beans (e.g. haricot, flageolet, red kidney, borlotti)

14oz/400g tin chopped tomatoes

4oz/100g courgette, chopped

4oz/100g red pepper, chopped

2oz/50g button mushrooms, wiped and halved

1 onion, peeled and chopped

1 celery stick, trimmed and finely sliced

2 garlic cloves, crushed

5 fl.oz/150ml water

1 tablespoon olive oil

1 rounded teaspoon herbes de Provence

1 teaspoon sun-dried tomato paste

1 bay leaf

black pepper

grated vegan 'cheese'

chopped black olives

Heat the oil in a large pan and fry the onion, celery and garlic until soft. Add the remaining ingredients apart from the 'cheese' and olives, and stir well. Bring to the boil, cover and simmer, stirring occasionally, for 15-20 minutes until the vegetables are cooked. Ladle the soup into bowls and garnish with the grated 'cheese' and chopped olives.

Puy lentil and mushroom soup (serves 4)

6oz/175g puy lentils

6oz/175g mushrooms, wiped and chopped

1 onion, peeled and finely chopped

2 garlic cloves, crushed

36 fl.oz/1075ml boiling vegetable stock

1 tablespoon olive oil

1 bay leaf

1 teaspoon dried thyme

1 teaspoon dried parsley

black pepper

chopped fresh parsley

Soak the lentils in the boiling stock for 1 hour. Fry the onion and garlic in the oil in a large saucepan until soft, then add the mushrooms and fry until the juices begin to run. Stir in the lentils, together with the soaking stock, bay leaf, thyme and dried parsley, season with black pepper and bring to the boil. Cover and simmer, stirring occasionally, for 35 minutes. Remove from the heat and allow to cool slightly. Pour half of the soup into a blender and blend smooth, then pour it back into the remaining soup and stir well. Reheat and garnish each bowl of soup with chopped fresh parsley.

Vichyssoise (serves 4)

12oz/350g leek, trimmed and sliced

6oz/175g potato, peeled and diced

1 onion, peeled and finely chopped

1oz/25g vegan margarine

18 fl.oz/550ml vegetable stock

6 fl.oz/175ml soya milk

1 bouquet garni

black pepper

chopped fresh chives

Melt the margarine in a large pan and gently fry the leek and onion for 5 minutes. Add the potato, stock and bouquet garni and season with black pepper. Stir well and bring to the boil, then cover and simmer for 20 minutes, stirring occasionally. Allow to cool slightly, remove the bouquet garni and pour the soup into a blender. Add the soya milk and blend smooth. Refrigerate for a few hours until cold. Ladle the soup into bowls and garnish with chopped fresh chives.

Aubergine and tomato soup (serves 4)

12oz/350g aubergine, finely chopped

12oz/350g ripe tomatoes, skinned and finely chopped

1 onion, peeled and finely chopped

2 garlic cloves, crushed

2 tablespoons olive oil

1 tablespoon finely chopped fresh basil

1 tablespoon finely chopped fresh oregano

1 dessertspoon tomato purée

1 teaspoon sugar

1 bay leaf

black pepper

12 fl.oz/350ml vegetable stock

vegan 'Parmesan'

chopped fresh parsley

Fry the aubergine, onion and garlic in the oil for 10 minutes, stirring frequently to prevent sticking. Add the tomato, basil, oregano, tomato purée, sugar, bay leaf and stock and season with black pepper. Stir well and bring to the boil. Cover and simmer for about 15 minutes, stirring occasionally until the vegetables are tender and the soup is thick. Serve in bowls, sprinkled with 'Parmesan' and garnished with chopped parsley.

Breton onion soup (serves 4)

1lb/450g onions, peeled and sliced

8oz/225g potato, peeled and diced

1oz/25g vegan margarine

25 fl.oz/750ml vegetable stock

black pepper

1 bay leaf

4 slices of garlic bread

grated vegan 'cheese'

Fry the onions in the margarine for 20 minutes. Add the potato, stock and bay leaf and season with black pepper, stir well and bring to the boil. Cover and simmer for about 15 minutes until the potato is done. Ladle the soup into bowls and top each with a slice of garlic bread. Sprinkle with grated 'cheese' and place under a hot grill until it just starts to melt.

Pistou (serves 4)

12oz/350g ripe tomatoes, skinned and chopped

8oz/225g courgette, diced

8oz/225g potato, peeled and diced

8oz/225g cooked haricot beans

4oz/100g carrot, scraped and diced

2oz/50g fennel, chopped

1 onion, peeled and chopped

2oz/50g small pasta shapes

1 tablespoon olive oil

1 dessertspoon tomato purée

15 fl.oz/450ml vegetable stock

black pepper

fresh basil leaves

pistou

4 tablespoons chopped fresh basil

2 garlic cloves

4 tablespoons olive oil

2 tablespoons vegan 'Parmesan'

Heat the tablespoonful of olive oil in a large pan and fry the onion and fennel for 5 minutes. Add the tomatoes and cook until pulpy. Stir in the stock, courgette, potato, carrot and tomato purée, season with black pepper and bring to the boil. Cover and simmer for 10 minutes, then add the haricot beans and pasta and bring back to the boil. Cover and simmer for another 10-15 minutes, stirring occasionally, until the vegetables are tender.

Meanwhile, blend the ingredients for the pistou together until smooth. Stir the pistou into the soup just before it is ready. Garnish each bowl of soup with a fresh basil leaf when serving.

Creamy cauliflower and almond soup (serves 4)

8oz/225g cauliflower, chopped

2 shallots, peeled and finely chopped

1 celery stick, trimmed and sliced

2oz/50g ground almonds

1 dessertspoon olive oil

24 fl.oz/725ml vegetable stock

6 fl.oz/175ml soya milk

1 bay leaf

black pepper

toasted flaked almonds

Gently fry the shallots and celery in the oil for 5 minutes. Add the cauliflower, ground almonds, vegetable stock and bay leaf, season with black pepper and stir well. Bring to the boil, cover and simmer, stirring occasionally, for about

15 minutes until the cauliflower is done. Allow to cool slightly, then transfer to a blender and blend until smooth. Pour back into the rinsed out pan and stir in the soya milk. Reheat and serve the bowls of soup garnished with toasted flaked almonds.

Chilled tomato and tarragon soup (serves 4)

> 1lb/450g ripe tomatoes, skinned and chopped
> 1 onion, peeled and chopped
> 2 garlic cloves, crushed
> 1 rounded dessertspoon vegan margarine
> 20 fl.oz/600ml vegetable stock
> 2 tablespoons finely chopped fresh tarragon
> 1 dessertspoon tomato purée
> 1 bay leaf
> black pepper
> finely sliced spring onions

Melt the margarine and soften the onion and garlic for 5 minutes. Add the tomatoes and cook until pulpy. Stir in the stock, tarragon, tomato purée and bay leaf and season with black pepper. Bring to the boil, cover and simmer for 15 minutes. Allow to cool slightly, then blend smooth. Keep in the fridge for a few hours until cold. Garnish with spring onions to serve.

Mushroom and wine soup (serves 4)

> 8oz/225g mushrooms, wiped and chopped
> 1 onion, peeled and chopped
> 2 garlic cloves, crushed
> 1 tablespoon olive oil
> 2 tablespoons chopped fresh parsley

16 fl.oz/475ml vegetable stock

4 fl.oz/125ml white wine

black pepper

extra chopped fresh parsley

Heat the oil and fry the onion and garlic until soft, then add the mushrooms and fry until the juices run. Stir in the stock, white wine and parsley and season with black pepper. Bring to the boil, cover and simmer for 10 minutes. Allow to cool, then blend smooth. Reheat in the cleaned pan and serve each bowl of soup garnished with chopped fresh parsley.

Watercress soup (serves 4)

2 bunches of watercress, trimmed and chopped

10oz/300g potato, peeled and diced

1 onion, peeled and chopped

1 dessertspoon olive oil

22 fl.oz/650ml vegetable stock

3 fl.oz/75ml soya milk

1 bay leaf

1 teaspoon dried chervil

black pepper

Fry the onion in the oil until softened. Add the remaining ingredients except the soya milk, and stir well. Bring to the boil, cover and simmer gently for about 15 minutes until the potato is cooked. Allow to cool slightly, remove the bay leaf and blend the soup until smooth. Pour back into the rinsed out pan, stir in the soya milk and reheat.

Herby green lentil soup (serves 4)

> 6oz/175g green lentils
>
> 6oz/175g green pepper, finely chopped
>
> 4oz/100g ripe tomato, skinned and chopped
>
> 1 celery stick, trimmed and finely sliced
>
> 1 onion, peeled and finely chopped
>
> 2 garlic cloves, crushed
>
> 30 fl.oz/900ml vegetable stock
>
> 4 rounded tablespoons finely chopped mixed fresh herbs (e.g.
>   oregano, thyme, basil, marjoram)
>
> 1 tablespoon olive oil
>
> 1 bay leaf
>
> black pepper
>
> grated vegan 'cheese'
>
> fresh parsley sprigs

Soak the lentils in the vegetable stock for an hour and a half. Fry the green pepper, celery, onion and garlic in the oil in a large saucepan for 5 minutes, add the tomatoes and cook until pulpy. Now add the lentils and stock, chopped herbs and bay leaf. Season with black pepper and stir well. Bring to the boil, cover and simmer, stirring occasionally, for about 40 minutes until the lentils are tender. Allow to cool slightly, then blend half of the mixture and stir this into the remaining soup in the pan. Reheat and garnish each bowl of soup with grated 'cheese' and a parsley sprig.

Celery and potato soup (serves 4)

> 8oz/225g celery, trimmed and chopped
>
> 8oz/225g potato, peeled and diced
>
> 1 onion, peeled and finely chopped
>
> 1 tablespoon olive oil
>
> 20 fl.oz/600ml vegetable stock

4 fl.oz/125ml soya milk

1 rounded teaspoon dried parsley

1 bay leaf

black pepper

fresh celery leaves

Fry the celery and onion in the oil for 10 minutes. Add the potato, vegetable stock, parsley and bay leaf and season with black pepper. Stir well and bring to the boil, then cover and simmer for about 20 minutes until the vegetables are done. Allow to cool slightly, remove the bay leaf and blend the soup smooth. Pour back into the cleaned pan, stir in the soya milk and reheat. Serve garnished with celery leaves.

Courgette and fennel soup (serves 4)

8oz/225g courgette

6oz/175g fennel, chopped

1 onion, peeled and chopped

1 garlic clove, crushed

1 tablespoon olive oil

20 fl.oz/600ml vegetable stock

1 teaspoon dried tarragon

1 teaspoon dried chervil

black pepper

fresh fennel leaves

Fry the fennel, onion and garlic in the oil for 10 minutes. Keep 2oz/50g courgette for garnish and chop the rest. Add the chopped courgette to the pan together with the stock, tarragon and chervil, season with black pepper and stir well. Bring to the boil, cover and simmer for 20 minutes. Allow to cool slightly, pour into a blender and blend smooth. Cut the remaining courgette into julienne strips and steam until just tender. Reheat the soup and garnish each bowl with the julienne strips and fresh fennel leaves.

LIGHT MEALS

With the main meal taken at either midday or in the evening and often consisting of three or four courses, lunch or supper dishes tend to be lighter. Open or closed toasted sandwiches are popular snacks, as are pan bagna, *short or long crusty rolls, split open and drizzled with* 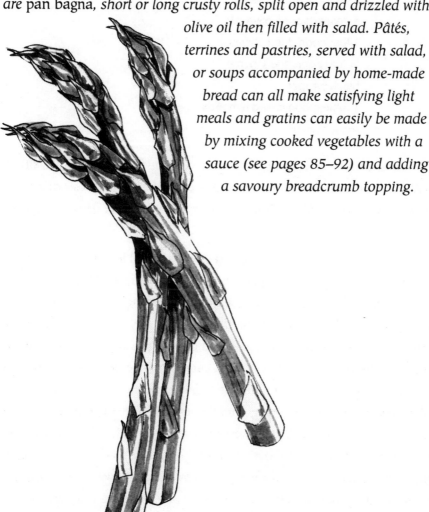 *olive oil then filled with salad. Pâtés, terrines and pastries, served with salad, or soups accompanied by home-made bread can all make satisfying light meals and gratins can easily be made by mixing cooked vegetables with a sauce (see pages 85–92) and adding a savoury breadcrumb topping.*

Aubergine, mushroom and almond charlotte (serves 4/6)

12oz/350g aubergine

4oz/100g mushrooms, wiped and finely chopped

4oz/100g ground almonds

4oz/100g breadcrumbs

1 onion, peeled and finely chopped

2 garlic cloves, crushed

1 dessertspoon olive oil

1 teaspoon dried chives

½ teaspoon dried thyme

black pepper

1 tablespoon flaked almonds

extra olive oil

Cut the aubergine in half lengthwise and score the flesh inside. Brush all over with olive oil and bake in a preheated oven at 180°C/350°F/Gas mark 4 for about 35 minutes until the flesh is tender. Scoop out the flesh and mash it. Keep the skin.

Fry the onion and garlic in the dessertspoonful of oil for 5 minutes. Add the mushrooms and fry until the juices begin to run. Remove from the heat and add the mashed aubergine, ground almonds, breadcrumbs, chives and thyme, season with black pepper and mix thoroughly. Line a 6 inch/15cm diameter ramekin dish with foil and grease. Use the aubergine skin to line the sides of the dish (smooth side on the outside), cutting it as necessary so that no gaps remain. Sprinkle the flaked almonds evenly over the base, then spoon the filling into the lined dish, being careful not to dislodge the skin. Press down firmly and evenly and fold any overhanging skin over the filling. Cover with foil and bake in a preheated oven at 180°C/350°F/Gas mark 4 for 30 minutes, then remove the foil and bake for 15 minutes more. Allow to cool in the dish for 15 minutes. Carefully invert the charlotte onto a serving plate and put it in the fridge until cold. Cut into wedges with a sharp knife to serve.

Tomato and olive croustade (serves 4)

base

4oz/100g breadcrumbs

2oz/50g mixed nuts, grated

1oz/25g vegan margarine

1 small onion, peeled and grated

1 garlic clove, crushed

1 teaspoon dried parsley

2 tablespoons soya milk

topping

12oz/350g firm tomatoes, skinned and sliced

6 black olives, chopped

1 dessertspoon olive oil

black pepper

vegan 'Parmesan'

fresh basil leaves

Melt the margarine in a saucepan, add the onion and garlic and fry for 2 minutes. Remove from the heat and mix in the breadcrumbs, nuts and parsley. Add the soya milk, combine everything well and spoon the mixture into a greased 8 inch/20cm round loose-bottomed flan tin. Press down firmly and evenly and bake in a preheated oven at 180°C/350°F/Gas mark 4 for 10 minutes.

Arrange the tomato slices in a circular overlapping pattern on top to cover completely. Scatter the chopped olives over and season with black pepper. Drizzle the olive oil over the top and sprinkle with 'Parmesan'. Return to the oven for 20 minutes more. Carefully remove from the tin, cut into 4 equal wedges and garnish each wedge with fresh basil leaves.

Ratatouille (serves 4/6)

1lb/450g aubergine, diced

12oz/350g courgette, sliced

8oz/225g red pepper, sliced

8oz/225g tomatoes, skinned and cut into wedges

4oz/100g button mushrooms, wiped and halved

1 onion, peeled and sliced

4 garlic cloves, sliced

4 tablespoons olive oil

2 bay leaves

2 rounded tablespoons chopped fresh basil

black pepper

finely chopped fresh parsley

Heat the oil in a large pan and fry the aubergine, red pepper, onion and garlic for 15 minutes, stirring frequently. Add the courgette, bay leaves and basil and season with black pepper. Continue cooking for 5 minutes, then add the mushrooms and tomatoes. Cook for another 5 minutes or so until the vegetables are done. Transfer to a warmed serving dish and garnish with fresh chopped parsley.

Broccoli and pasta amande (serves 4)

1lb/450g broccoli, chopped

4oz/100g pasta spirals

2oz/50g ground almonds

1oz/25g flaked almonds

½oz/15g cornflour

1 onion, peeled and finely chopped

1 garlic clove, crushed

1 dessertspoon olive oil

1 teaspoon dried chervil

black pepper

10 fl.oz/300ml vegetable stock

12 fl.oz/350ml soya milk

Fry the onion and garlic in the oil until soft, then add the broccoli, stock and chervil and stir well. Bring to the boil, cover and simmer until the broccoli is just tender. Meanwhile, cook the pasta until just done. Dissolve the cornflour in the soya milk and add to the broccoli, together with the ground almonds. Season with black pepper and bring to the boil whilst stirring. Continue stirring for a minute or so until the sauce thickens. Drain the pasta and add to the sauce. Mix well, then divide between 4 individual warmed serving dishes. Sprinkle the flaked almonds on top and place under a hot grill for a couple of minutes until golden brown.

Asparagus and mushroom gratin (serves 4)

1lb/450g asparagus, trimmed and cut into 1 inch/2.5cm lengths

4oz/100g mushrooms, wiped and finely chopped

1 garlic clove, crushed

1 dessertspoon olive oil

2 tablespoons finely chopped fresh parsley

9 fl.oz/250ml soya milk

½oz/15g cornflour

black pepper

topping

1oz/25g breadcrumbs

½oz/15g walnuts, finely chopped

1 rounded dessertspoon vegan 'Parmesan'

1 teaspoon dried chives

Heat the oil and gently fry the mushrooms and garlic until the juices begin to run. Dissolve the cornflour in the soya milk and add to the pan, together with the parsley. Season with black pepper and stir well. Bring to the boil whilst stirring and continue stirring for a minute or so until the sauce thickens, then remove from the heat. Steam the asparagus until just tender and add to the sauce. Mix well and transfer to a warmed ovenproof serving dish. Mix the topping ingredients together and sprinkle evenly over the top. Bake in a preheated oven at 170°C/325°F/Gas mark 3 for 20 minutes until golden.

Cauliflower and tomato gratin (serves 4)

12oz/350g cauliflower, cut into small florets

8oz/225g ripe tomatoes, skinned and chopped

1 onion, peeled and finely chopped

2 garlic cloves, crushed

1 tablespoon olive oil

1 dessertspoon tomato purée

1 rounded tablespoon chopped fresh chervil

pinch of cayenne pepper

black pepper

topping

1oz/25g breadcrumbs

1oz/25g vegan 'cheese', grated

1 teaspoon dried chives

Mix the breadcrumbs with the grated 'cheese' and chives. Heat the oil and gently soften the onion and garlic. Add the tomatoes, tomato purée, chervil and cayenne pepper and season with black pepper. Cook until the tomatoes are pulpy and the sauce thickens. Meanwhile, steam the cauliflower until tender. Add to the hot tomato sauce, spoon into a warmed ovenproof serving dish and sprinkle evenly with the topping. Place under a medium hot grill for about 10 minutes until browned.

Hazelnut, rice and ratatouille flan (serves 4)

flan case

4oz/100g long grain rice

2oz/50g hazelnuts, grated

2oz/50g breadcrumbs

1 tablespoon hazelnut butter

3 tablespoons water

olive oil

filling

6oz/175g courgette, chopped

4oz/100g red pepper, chopped

4oz/100g tomato, skinned and chopped

2oz/50g mushrooms, wiped and chopped

1 small red onion, peeled and chopped

2 garlic cloves, crushed

1 tablespoon olive oil

1 rounded tablespoon finely chopped fresh basil

1 bay leaf

black pepper

½oz/15g hazelnuts, chopped

Cook the rice, drain and rinse under cold running water. Drain well and put in a large bowl, and mix in the hazelnuts and breadcrumbs. Combine the hazelnut butter with the water until smooth, add to the rice mixture and stir thoroughly. Spoon the mixture into a greased 8 inch/20cm diameter loose-bottomed flan tin. Press out evenly to cover the base and sides of the tin, to make a flan case. Brush with oil and bake blind in a preheated oven at 180°C/350°F/Gas mark 4 for 10 minutes.

Heat the oil for the filling and fry the onion and garlic until softened. Add the courgette, red pepper, bay leaf and basil and season with black pepper. Fry for 5 minutes more, stirring occasionally. Finally add the mushrooms and tomato and continue stirring around for 2 minutes. Spoon the filling into the flan case and sprinkle the hazelnuts on top. Cover with foil and return to the oven for 25 minutes, then remove the foil and bake for another 5-10 minutes until golden. Run a sharp knife around the edges to loosen, carefully remove from the tin and cut into wedges.

'Cheesy' grilled potatoes with peppers (serves 4)

1½lb/675g new potatoes, scraped

12oz/350g ripe tomatoes, skinned and chopped

3oz/75g red pepper, thinly sliced

3oz/75g green pepper, thinly sliced

3oz/75g yellow pepper, thinly sliced

1 red onion, peeled and finely chopped

1 tablespoon olive oil

1 dessertspoon tomato purée

2 fl.oz/50ml water

½ teaspoon paprika

½ teaspoon thyme

1 teaspoon dried basil

pinch of ground bay leaves

black pepper

1½oz/40g vegan 'cheese', grated

finely chopped fresh parsley

Heat the oil and fry the onion and peppers until soft. Add the tomatoes, tomato purée, water, paprika, thyme, basil and ground bay leaves, season with black pepper and stir well. Bring to the boil and simmer gently for 5-10 minutes until the sauce thickens and the peppers are tender. Boil the potatoes, drain and dice and add to the hot sauce. Mix well, transfer to a warmed oven-proof serving dish and sprinkle the grated 'cheese' on top. Place under a hot grill for a minute or two until the 'cheese' begins to melt. Garnish with chopped parsley just before serving.

MAIN COURSES

Country-style stews and casseroles are especially popular in rural areas, where they are made with home-grown vegetables or seasonally available produce from market gardens or the local market. These dishes are often enriched with locally produced cider or wine, which gives both a wonderful flavour and a lovely aroma. The names of some recipes are derived from the type of dish they are cooked in. Examples are cassoulet – a deep earthenware pot used extensively in Gascony, and tian – a shallow square or rectangular earthenware dish which is popular in Provence.

Country cider casserole (serves 4)

12oz/350g leek, trimmed and sliced

12oz/350g carrot, scraped and chopped

8oz/225g turnip, peeled and diced

4oz/100g soup mix (e.g. a mixture of lentils, barley, wheatgrain, split peas)

2oz/50g dried apricots, finely chopped

1 eating apple, peeled, cored and chopped

1 onion, peeled and chopped

2 garlic cloves, crushed

20 fl.oz/600ml boiling vegetable stock

12 fl.oz/350ml cider

2 tablespoons olive oil

1 bay leaf

1 teaspoon paprika

1 rounded dessertspoon dried fines herbes

black pepper

finely chopped fresh chervil

chopped walnuts

Soak the soup mix in the vegetable stock for an hour, then bring to the boil, cover and simmer for 20 minutes. Heat the oil in a large pan and fry the leek, onion and garlic for 10 minutes. Add the soup mix and remaining stock, together with the rest of the ingredients apart from the chervil and walnuts. Stir well and bring to the boil. Simmer for 5 minutes, then transfer to a deep casserole dish. Cover and bake in a preheated oven at 170°C/325°F/Gas mark 3 for 1 hour. Garnish with chopped chervil and walnuts and serve with a plain green vegetable and garlic bread.

Celeriac and mixed bean provençale (serves 4)

12oz/350g ripe tomatoes, skinned and chopped

6oz/175g mixed cooked beans (e.g. haricot, flageolet, red kidney)

6oz/175g French beans, topped, tailed and cut into ½inch/1cm
   lengths

2oz/50g fennel, finely chopped

1 onion, peeled and finely chopped

2 garlic cloves, crushed

2 tablespoons water

1 tablespoon olive oil

1 dessertspoon tomato purée

1 rounded teaspoon herbes de Provence

1 bay leaf

black pepper

 topping

1½lb/675g peeled celeriac, diced

squeeze of lemon juice

2 tablespoons vegan margarine

2 tablespoons soya milk

½oz/15g breadcrumbs

½oz/15g walnuts, finely chopped

1 teaspoon dried chives

Heat the oil in a large pan and fry the fennel, onion and garlic for about 10 minutes until soft. Add the tomatoes and fry until pulpy, then stir in the mixed cooked beans, water, tomato purée, herbes de Provence and bay leaf. Season with black pepper and bring to the boil, cover and simmer, stirring occasionally, for 10 minutes. Meanwhile, steam the French beans until just tender. Add to the pan, mix in well, and spoon everything into a greased shallow baking dish.

Put the celeriac in a large pan of water and add a squeeze of lemon juice. Bring to the boil and simmer until done. Drain and dry off over a low heat. Mash the celeriac with the margarine, stir in the soya milk and mix well. Spread evenly over the vegetables in the baking dish. Mix the breadcrumbs with the walnuts and chives and sprinkle on top. Cover with foil and bake in a preheated oven at 170°C/325°F/Gas mark 3 for 25 minutes. Uncover and bake for 5 minutes more until golden brown. Serve with vegetables or salad.

Cauliflower and mushroom croustade (serves 4)

croustade

2oz/50g ground almonds

2oz/50g porridge oats

2oz/50g fine oatmeal

2oz/50g breadcrumbs

1oz/25g vegan margarine

½oz/15g flaked almonds

2 rounded tablespoons vegan 'Parmesan'

2 teaspoons dried chives

filling

1lb/450g cauliflower, cut into small florets

6oz/175g mushrooms, wiped and chopped

4oz/100g tomato, chopped

1 onion, peeled and finely chopped

1 dessertspoon olive oil

14 fl.oz/400ml soya milk

½oz/15g cornflour

1oz/25g vegan 'cheese', grated

1 rounded teaspoon Dijon mustard

2 teaspoons dried parsley

black pepper

Melt the margarine over a low heat. Remove from the heat, add the rest of the croustade ingredients and mix thoroughly. Steam the cauliflower until just tender. Heat the oil in a saucepan and gently soften the onion, then add the mushrooms and fry for 1 minute more. Mix the cornflour and mustard with the soya milk until smooth and add to the pan together with the parsley and 'cheese'. Season with black pepper and bring to the boil while stirring. Continue stirring for a minute or so until the sauce thickens, then remove from the heat and stir in the cauliflower and tomato.

Spoon half of the croustade mixture into a greased shallow casserole dish and press it down evenly. Spread the filling on top and sprinkle the rest of the croustade mixture over the filling. Cover with foil and bake in a preheated oven at 180°C/350°F/Gas mark 4 for 25 minutes, then take off the foil and bake for another 5 minutes or so until golden brown. Serve with a potato dish.

Herby vegetable and chickpea stew (serves 4)

6oz/175g cooked chickpeas

6oz/175g courgette, halved lengthwise and sliced

6oz/175g cauliflower, cut into small florets

6oz/175g red pepper, chopped

6oz/175g carrot, scraped and chopped

4oz/100g button mushrooms, wiped and halved

4oz/100g shallots, peeled and sliced

2 garlic cloves, crushed

1 celery stick, trimmed and finely sliced

14oz/400g tin chopped tomatoes

5 fl.oz/150ml vegetable stock

1 tablespoon olive oil

4 tablespoons finely chopped mixed fresh herbs (e.g. thyme, rosemary, basil, oregano, marjoram)

1 bay leaf

1 teaspoon fennel seed

pinch of cayenne pepper

black pepper

chopped fresh parsley

Fry the shallot, garlic and celery in the oil until softened. Add the remaining ingredients except the fresh parsley and chickpeas and stir well. Bring to the boil, cover and simmer gently, stirring occasionally, for 20 minutes. Add the chickpeas, stir well and continue simmering for another 10 minutes until the vegetables are done and the mixture is thick. Serve on a bed of rice, garnished with fresh parsley.

Courgette, mushroom and rice tian (serves 4)

8oz/225g courgette, grated

6oz/175g mushrooms, wiped and finely chopped

6oz/175g long grain rice

4oz/100g breadcrumbs

1oz/25g soya flour

1 onion, peeled and finely chopped

2 garlic cloves, crushed

4 tablespoons water

1 tablespoon olive oil

1 rounded tablespoon vegan 'Parmesan'

1 rounded teaspoon dried thyme

pinch of ground bay leaves

black pepper

1 tomato, sliced

extra olive oil

dried parsley

Cook the rice and drain. Heat the tablespoonful of oil in a large pan and gently fry the onion and garlic until soft. Add the mushrooms and fry until the juices begin to run, then remove from the heat and add the rice, courgette, breadcrumbs, 'Parmesan', thyme and ground bay leaves. Season with black pepper and combine well. Mix the soya flour with the water until smooth and stir into the mixture. Spoon everything into a greased shallow rectangular baking dish and press down firmly and evenly. Brush the top with olive oil and arrange the tomato slices on top. Brush these lightly with oil as well and sprinkle with parsley. Bake in a preheated oven at 180°C/350°F/Gas mark 4 for 30 minutes until browned. Serve with warm bread and vegetables.

Root vegetable cassoulet (serves 4)

2lb/900g peeled root vegetables (e.g. celeriac, turnip, carrot, potato), cut into even-sized chunks

14oz/400g tin chopped tomatoes

10oz/300g cooked haricot beans

8 baby onions, peeled and halved

2 garlic cloves, crushed

1 tablespoon olive oil

1 dessertspoon tomato purée

1 bouquet garni

black pepper

2 fl.oz/50ml white wine

6 fl.oz/175ml vegetable stock

1oz/25g breadcrumbs

Fry the onion and garlic in the oil for a couple of minutes. Add the remaining ingredients, except the breadcrumbs, and stir well. Bring to the boil, cover and simmer for 5 minutes. Transfer to an ovenproof earthenware dish and sprinkle the breadcrumbs on top. Cover and bake in a preheated oven at 170°C/325°F/Gas mark 3 for 1 hour. Stir the breadcrumbs into the casserole, cover and return to the oven for 15 minutes. Serve with warm crusty bread and a green salad.

Layered cabbage gratin (serves 4)

1¼lb/550 white cabbage leaves

filling

12oz/350g ripe tomatoes, skinned and chopped

8oz/225g mushrooms, wiped and finely chopped

8oz/225g carrot, scraped and grated

4oz/100g red pepper, finely sliced

2 celery sticks, trimmed and finely sliced

1 onion, peeled and finely chopped

2 garlic cloves, crushed

1oz/25g natural minced textured vegetable protein

1 tablespoon olive oil

2 fl.oz/50ml white wine

1 dessertspoon tomato purée

1 rounded tablespoon finely chopped fresh basil

1 rounded tablespoon finely chopped fresh oregano

pinch of ground bay leaves

black pepper

topping

1½oz/40g breadcrumbs

2 tablespoons vegan 'Parmesan'

1 rounded tablespoon pine kernels, grated

1 rounded teaspoon dried parsley

Put the tomatoes, wine, tomato purée, vegetable protein, basil, oregano and ground bay leaves in a mixing bowl and combine. Cover and leave to stand for 30 minutes.

Heat the oil in a pan and gently fry the onion, garlic and celery until softened. Add the mushrooms, carrot and red pepper and the tomato mixture and stir well. Season with black pepper and bring to the boil. Cover and simmer, stirring occasionally, for 5-10 minutes until the vegetables are tender, then remove from the heat.

Cut the thick centre stalks from the cabbage leaves and discard. Put the leaves into a large saucepan and cover with water. Bring to the boil, cover and simmer for 5 minutes. Drain the leaves thoroughly, then spread half of them in a greased baking dish of about 10 x 14 inches/25 x 35cm. Spread half the filling evenly over the leaves, then repeat these layers.

Mix the topping ingredients and sprinkle evenly over the top. Cover with foil and bake in a preheated oven at 180°C/350°F/Gas mark 4 for 30 minutes. Remove the foil and bake for a further 5-10 minutes until browned. Serve with warm bread and salad.

Provençal rice stew (serves 4)

1lb/450g ripe tomatoes, skinned and chopped

6oz/175g red rice

6oz/175g turnip, peeled and cut into julienne strips

6oz/175g carrot, scraped and cut into julienne strips

6oz/175g courgette, chopped

4oz/100g red pepper, finely sliced

4oz/100g mushrooms, wiped and chopped

2oz/50g fennel, finely sliced

1 onion, peeled and finely chopped

4 garlic cloves, crushed

1 tablespoon olive oil

22 fl.oz/650ml vegetable stock

1 dessertspoon tomato purée

1 rounded teaspoon herbes de Provence

½ teaspoon fennel seed

1 bay leaf

black pepper

capers

grated vegan 'cheese'

Heat the oil in a large pan and fry the onion, fennel and garlic for 5 minutes. Add the rice, vegetable stock and tomato purée and stir well. Bring to the boil, cover and simmer for 15 minutes, then add the tomatoes and simmer for 5 minutes more until the tomatoes are soft. Now add the vegetables, herbes de Provence, fennel seed and bay leaf and season with black pepper. Stir well and bring to the boil. Cover and simmer, stirring occasionally, for 30-35 minutes until the mixture is thick and the rice and vegetables are cooked. Garnish with capers and grated 'cheese' and serve with warm crusty bread and salad.

Savoury baked buckwheat pancakes (serves 4)

pancakes
3oz/75g buckwheat flour

1oz/25g plain flour

10 fl.oz/300ml soya milk

2 tablespoons water

vegan margarine

filling
12oz/350g aubergine, finely chopped

8oz/225g tomatoes, skinned and chopped

3 tablespoons olive oil

1 onion, peeled and finely chopped

2 garlic cloves, crushed

1 tablespoon red wine

1 rounded tablespoon finely chopped fresh basil

1 dessertspoon tomato purée

½ teaspoon paprika

black pepper

topping
3oz/75g mushrooms, wiped and finely chopped

1 garlic clove, crushed

1 dessertspoon olive oil

4 fl.oz/125ml soya milk

1 dessertspoon cornflour

1 rounded teaspoon dried parsley

black pepper

1oz/25g breadcrumbs

First make the pancakes. Whisk all the ingredients apart from the margarine together and leave to stand for 15 minutes. Lightly grease a 7 inch/18cm non-stick frying pan with margarine and heat until hot. Whisk the batter again, then use just over 2 tablespoonfuls to make a pancake. Repeat with the remaining batter, making 8 pancakes in all. Stack them on a plate, cover and set aside.

Fry the aubergine, onion and garlic in the oil for 10 minutes, stirring frequently to prevent sticking. Add the remaining filling ingredients and continue cooking for 10-15 minutes until the mixture is thick. Allow to cool slightly, then divide the filling equally between the pancakes. Roll each pancake up to enclose the filling and put them in a 10 x 7 inch/25 x 20cm greased baking dish.

Heat the oil for the topping and gently fry the mushrooms and garlic until the juices run from the mushrooms. Dissolve the cornflour in the soya milk and add to the pan together with the parsley. Season with black pepper and stir well. Bring to the boil while stirring and continue stirring until the sauce thickens. Spoon the sauce evenly over the filled pancakes and sprinkle the breadcrumbs on the top. Cover with foil and bake in a preheated oven at 180°C/350°F/Gas mark 4 for 25 minutes, then remove the foil and bake for another 10 minutes until golden brown. Serve with vegetables or a salad.

Chestnut and mushroom bourguignon (serves 4)

12oz/350g peeled fresh chestnuts

12oz/350g chestnut mushrooms, wiped and quartered

12oz/350g shallots, peeled and halved

2oz/50g natural textured vegetable protein chunks

½oz/15g dried mushrooms

22 fl.oz/650ml vegetable stock

5 fl.oz/150ml red wine

4 garlic cloves, crushed

2 rounded dessertspoons cornflour

1 tablespoon olive oil

few sprigs of fresh thyme

2 bay leaves

black pepper

chopped fresh parsley

Keep 4 fl.oz/125ml of the vegetable stock and put the rest into a bowl with the red wine. Add the vegetable protein and dried mushrooms and leave to soak for 1 hour.

Heat the oil in a large pan and fry the shallots and garlic for 5 minutes. Add the vegetable protein and mushrooms and the soaking liquid, together with the chestnuts, thyme and bay leaves. Season with black pepper and stir well, then bring to the boil, cover and simmer for 10 minutes. Dissolve the cornflour in the remaining stock and add it to the pan with the chestnut mushrooms. Stir well and transfer to a casserole dish, cover and bake in a preheated oven at 170°C/325°F/Gas mark 3 for 1 hour. Garnish with chopped fresh parsley and serve with a rice dish and warm bread.

Butternut squash and barley casserole (serves 4)

1lb/450g butternut squash, peeled and diced

8oz/225g potato, peeled and diced

8oz/225g leek, trimmed and sliced

4oz/100g pot barley

1 onion, peeled and sliced

2 garlic cloves, crushed

20 fl.oz/600ml boiling water

10 fl.oz/300ml cold water

1 tablespoon olive oil

1 bay leaf

1 tablespoon vegan vegetable bouillon

1 dessertspoon dried fines herbes

½ teaspoon paprika

black pepper

grated vegan 'cheese'

chopped fresh parsley

Soak the barley in the boiling water for an hour, then bring to the boil and simmer for 10 minutes. Heat the oil in a large pan and fry the leek, onion and garlic until softened. Remove from the heat and add the barley and its remaining cooking liquid. Dissolve the bouillon in the cold water and add, together with the squash, potato, bay leaf, fines herbes and paprika. Season with black pepper and stir well. Spoon into a casserole dish, cover and bake in a preheated oven at 170°C/325°F/Gas mark 3 for 1¼ hours. Sprinkle the top with grated 'cheese' and garnish with parsley. Serve with a green vegetable and warm bread.

Aubergine and mushroom ragoût (serves 4)

1¼lb/550g aubergine, diced

8oz/225g tomatoes, skinned and chopped

6oz/175g mushrooms, wiped and sliced

2oz/50g natural textured vegetable protein chunks

½oz/15g dried mushrooms

2 red onions, peeled and chopped

4 garlic cloves, crushed

18 fl.oz/550ml boiling vegetable stock

2 fl.oz/50ml red wine

4 tablespoons olive oil

1 bouquet garni

1 rounded dessertspoon arrowroot

1 tablespoon water

black pepper

chopped fresh parsley

Soak the dried mushrooms and vegetable protein in the boiled vegetable stock for 1 hour. Fry the aubergine, onion and garlic in the oil for 10 minutes, stirring occasionally to prevent sticking, then put in the tomatoes and cook for 5 minutes until they are pulpy. Add the mushrooms and vegetable protein with the remaining stock, as well as the sliced mushrooms, wine and bouquet garni. Season with black pepper and stir well. Bring to the boil, cover and simmer, stirring occasionally, for 30 minutes. Dissolve the arrowroot in the water and add to the pan. Bring to the boil while stirring, then transfer to a warmed serving dish and garnish with chopped parsley. Serve with rice and crusty bread.

SAVOURY PASTRIES

Even the smallest town in France will have at least one pâtisserie, a specialist shop selling cakes and all kinds of pastry dishes, both sweet and savoury. Puff pastry is believed to have been invented by a pastry cook in the Alsace-Lorraine region in the 17th century and it remains as popular as ever today, especially for making vol-au-vent cases. Ready-made, frozen vol-au-vent cases suitable for vegans can easily be obtained from most supermarkets and these can be filled with savoury salad mixtures and served as starters or buffet food.

The pastries below can either be served with salad as a light meal or made into a more substantial meal when accompanied by vegetable and salad dishes. They also make an ideal choice when entertaining, as they can all be made in advance and frozen, then simply thawed and reheated when required.

Aubergine, lentil and walnut pâté en croûte (serves 4/6)

pastry

8oz/225g plain flour

2oz/50g vegan margarine, melted

1 teaspoon easy-blend yeast

½ teaspoon salt

approx. 4 fl.oz/125ml soya milk, warmed

extra soya milk

sesame seeds

filling

12oz/350g aubergine, finely chopped

4oz/100g puy lentils

2oz/50g walnuts, grated

2oz/50g breadcrumbs

1 onion, peeled and finely chopped

2 garlic cloves, crushed

4 tablespoons olive oil

1 tablespoon finely chopped fresh chives

black pepper

Put the flour, yeast and salt in a large bowl and stir together, then mix in the melted margarine. Gradually add the warmed soya milk until a soft dough forms, turn this out onto a floured board and knead well. Return to the bowl, cover and leave in a warm place for 1 hour.

Cook the lentils, drain and press out any excess water with the back of a spoon, and mash them. Fry the aubergine, onion and garlic in the oil for about 15 minutes, stirring occasionally to prevent sticking, until tender. Remove from the heat and add the lentils, walnuts, breadcrumbs and chives. Season with black pepper and mix thoroughly.

Turn the dough out onto a floured board and cut it into 2 equal portions. Roll out one piece to fit the base of a 9 x 7 inch/23 x 18cm greased baking dish. Spoon the filling evenly onto the pastry base and press down firmly. Roll the other piece of dough out to fit the top, put it over the filling and press down lightly. Score a diamond pattern on top with a sharp knife. Make a slit in the centre of each diamond, then allow to stand for 30 minutes. Brush the top with soya milk, sprinkle with sesame seeds, cover and bake in a preheated oven at 180°C/350°F/Gas mark 4 for 30 minutes. Uncover and bake for another 10 minutes or so until golden brown.

Spinach pies (serves 6)

6oz/175g puff pastry

soya milk

sesame seeds

filling

12oz/350g fresh spinach

1 onion, peeled and finely chopped

1 garlic clove, crushed

2oz/50g vegan 'cream cheese'

1 dessertspoon olive oil

½ teaspoon dried marjoram

black pepper

Wash the spinach leaves and put them in a saucepan with only the water that clings to them. Cover and cook gently until done, then drain and allow to cool. Squeeze out as much liquid as possible from the spinach and chop it finely. Fry the onion and garlic in the oil until soft, remove from the heat and add the spinach and remaining filling ingredients. Mix very well and leave to cool.

Divide the pastry into 6 equal portions. Shape each portion into a ball and roll these out on a floured board into 5 inch/13cm circles. Put the circles on a flat surface and divide the filling equally between them, placing it on one half of each circle only. Dampen the edges of the pastry with water and fold the pastry over the filling to enclose. Pinch the edges together, then place the pies on a greased baking sheet. Make a couple of slits in the top of each pie, brush them with soya milk and sprinkle with sesame seeds. Bake in a preheated oven at 170°C/325°F/Gas mark 3 for about 30 minutes until golden.

Flamiche (serves 4)

base
8oz/225g plain flour
½ sachet easy-blend yeast
½ teaspoon salt
1 tablespoon olive oil
approx. 4 fl.oz/125ml warm water

topping
1¼lb/550g leeks, trimmed
2 garlic cloves, crushed
1oz/25g vegan margarine
½ teaspoon dried thyme
black pepper
olive oil
grated vegan 'cheese'

Mix the flour, yeast and salt in a large bowl, stir in the olive oil and gradually add the water until a soft dough forms. Turn out onto a floured board and knead well. Roll out to a circle of 11 inches/28cm diameter and put this on a greased baking sheet. Cover with a piece of oiled cling film and leave in a warm place for 1 hour until risen.

Cut the leeks in half lengthwise, then cut into slices. Melt the margarine, add the leeks and garlic and fry, stirring occasionally, for 10 minutes. Remove from the heat and add the thyme. Season with black pepper and mix well.

Brush the base with olive oil and spoon the leeks evenly on top. Bake in a preheated oven at 180°C/350°F/Gas mark 4 for 25 minutes. Sprinkle the top with grated 'cheese' before serving.

Red onion, tomato and tarragon tarts (serves 4)

pastry
4oz/100g fine wholemeal self raising flour

1½oz/40g vegan margarine

water

filling
1lb/450g red onions, peeled and finely chopped

4oz/100g tomato, skinned and chopped

2 garlic cloves, crushed

1 tablespoon olive oil

1 dessertspoon sun-dried tomato paste

1 rounded tablespoon finely chopped fresh tarragon

black pepper

1 tomato, sliced

vegan 'Parmesan'

extra chopped fresh tarragon

Rub the margarine into the flour and add enough water to make a soft dough. Knead well, then divide the dough into 4 equal pieces and roll each one out on a floured board to fit a 4 inch/10cm diameter greased flan tin. Prick the bases and bake blind in a preheated oven at 180°C/350°F/Gas mark 4 for 5 minutes.

Heat the oil and fry the onion and garlic for 15 minutes, stirring occasionally. Add the chopped tomatoes, tablespoon of tarragon and tomato paste, season with black pepper and cook while stirring for 5 minutes. Divide the mixture evenly between the pastry cases, arrange the tomato slices on top and sprinkle with 'Parmesan'. Return to the oven for 25 minutes. Carefully remove the flans from the tins and garnish with fresh tarragon when serving.

Savoury palmiers (makes 12)

6oz/175g puff pastry

vegan 'Parmesan'

filling

4oz/100g red pepper, finely chopped

1 shallot, peeled and finely chopped

1 garlic clove, crushed

½oz/15g vegan 'cheese', grated

1 tablespoon sun-dried tomato paste

1 dessertspoon olive oil

1 rounded tablespoon finely chopped fresh mixed herbs

black pepper

Fry the red pepper, shallot and garlic in the oil for 5 minutes. Remove from the heat and add the 'cheese' and herbs, season with black pepper and mix well.

Roll out the pastry on a floured board into an oblong of 10 x 9 inches/25 x 23cm. Spread the tomato paste evenly over the pastry, leaving a ½ inch/1cm gap along the two longer edges. Spoon the filling over the tomato paste. Roll the two longer edges towards the centre to meet, dampen the edges with water and pinch together to join. Cut the roll into 12 equal slices and lay the slices flat, and spaced out to allow for spreading, on a greased baking sheet. Sprinkle with 'Parmesan' and bake in a preheated oven at 170°C/325°F/Gas mark 3 for about 30 minutes until golden.

Chestnut, lentil and prune plait (serves 4/6)

12oz/350g puff pastry

soya milk

sesame seeds

filling

4oz/100g dried chestnuts

4oz/100g puy lentils

4oz/100g carrot, scraped and grated

2oz/50g no-need-to-soak prunes, finely chopped

1 onion, peeled and finely chopped

1 garlic clove, crushed

1 tablespoon olive oil

1 rounded tablespoon finely chopped fresh chives

½ teaspoon paprika

black pepper

4 tablespoons soya milk

Soak the chestnuts in boiling water for an hour, drain and put in a pan of fresh water. Bring to the boil, cover and simmer for about 45 minutes until tender. Drain and grate the chestnuts. Cook the lentils, drain and press out any excess water with the back of a spoon. Mash them and add to the grated chestnuts. Fry the carrot, onion and garlic in the oil for 5 minutes, then add to the mixture together with the remaining filling ingredients and combine thoroughly.

Roll out the pastry on a floured board into a 12 inch/30cm square. Place the filling evenly along the centre, neatening it so it is no more than about 4½ inches/11.5cm wide. Make diagonal cuts in the pastry edges at ¾ inch/2cm intervals. Place alternate strips of pastry over the filling to give a plaited effect and to enclose the filling completely. Carefully transfer to a greased baking sheet and brush with soya milk. Sprinkle with sesame seeds and bake in a preheated oven at 170°C/325°F/Gas mark 3 for 35-40 minutes until golden brown.

Courgette lattice flan (serves 4)

pastry

8oz/225g fine wholemeal self raising flour

3oz/75g vegan margarine

¼ teaspoon cayenne pepper

water

filling

12oz/350g courgettes, finely sliced

6oz/175g tomatoes, skinned and chopped

1oz/25g vegan 'cheese', grated

1 small onion, peeled and finely chopped

1 garlic clove, crushed

1 dessertspoon olive oil

1 dessertspoon tomato purée

1 rounded tablespoon finely chopped fresh basil

½teaspoon celery seed

black pepper

Sift the flour with the cayenne pepper into a mixing bowl. Rub in the margarine, then gradually add enough water to make a soft dough. Roll out three-quarters of the dough on a floured board to line a greased 8 inch/20cm diameter deep loose-bottomed flan tin. Prick the base and bake blind in a preheated oven at 180°C/350°F/Gas mark 4 for 5 minutes. Roll out the remaining pastry thinly and cut into ¹/₂ inch/1cm wide strips for the lattice top.

Heat the oil and gently fry the onion and garlic until softened. Add the tomatoes, tomato purée, basil and celery seed and season with black pepper. Simmer for about 5 minutes until the tomatoes become pulpy and the mixture thickens, then add the courgettes and stir well. Raise the heat and simmer for 3 minutes, stirring occasionally. Remove from the heat and add the grated 'cheese'. Spoon the filling into the flan case and arrange the pastry strips in a lattice pattern on top. Put the flan back in the oven for 30-35 minutes until browned.

Pissaladière (serves 4)

base

8oz/225g plain flour

1 teaspoon easy-blend yeast

½ teaspoon salt

1 tablespoon olive oil

approx. 4 fl.oz/125ml warm water

topping

1lb/450g onions, peeled and sliced

2 garlic cloves, crushed

4 black olives, chopped

2 tablespoons olive oil

1 teaspoon herbes de Provence

black pepper

extra olive oil

finely chopped fresh parsley

Put the flour, yeast and salt in a bowl and mix. Stir in the olive oil, then gradually add the warm water until a soft dough forms. Knead the dough and return it to the bowl, then cover and leave in a warm place for 1 hour to rise. Knead the dough again and roll it out on a floured board into an oblong measuring 11 x 8 inches/28 x 20cm. Transfer to a greased baking sheet, cover and leave in a warm place for 30 minutes.

Fry the onions and garlic in the 2 tablespoonfuls of oil for 20 minutes, stirring occasionally, until soft. Remove from the heat and add the olives and herbs, season with black pepper and mix well. Brush the edges of the dough with olive oil and spread the onion mixture evenly on the top. Bake in a preheated oven at 200°C/400°F/Gas mark 6 for 15 minutes. Garnish with fresh chopped parsley and serve.

Sweet pepper and olive flan (serves 4)

pastry
6oz/175g fine wholemeal self raising flour

2½oz/65g vegan margarine

water

filling
12oz/350g mixed peppers

6oz/175g ripe tomatoes, skinned and chopped

2oz/50g black olives, chopped

1 onion, peeled and finely chopped

2 garlic cloves, crushed

1 tablespoon olive oil

2 rounded tablespoons finely chopped fresh basil

1 dessertspoon tomato purée

pinch of cayenne pepper

black pepper

fresh basil leaves

Rub the margarine into the flour and gradually add enough water to form a soft dough. Turn out onto a floured board and roll out to line a greased 8 inch/20cm diameter loose-bottomed flan tin. Prick the base with a fork and bake blind in a preheated oven at 180°C/350°F/Gas mark 4 for 10 minutes.

Put the peppers on a baking tray under a hot grill until the skins blister. Allow to cool slightly, then carefully remove the skins, stalks, membranes and seeds and chop the flesh.

Fry the onion and garlic in the oil until soft. Add the tomatoes, chopped basil, tomato purée and cayenne pepper, season with black pepper and stir well. Cook for about 10 minutes until the tomatoes are pulpy and the sauce thickens. Remove from the heat and mix in the chopped peppers and olives. Spoon the mixture evenly into the flan case and return the tin to the oven for 20 minutes. Garnish with fresh basil leaves.

ACCOMPANIMENTS

It may come as a surprise to find that the humble cabbage and potato are firm favourites and the French have literally dozens of ways of serving these two basic vegetables. Market stalls are often piled high with every available type of cabbage and they can be served very simply by braising, either on their own or in combination with other vegetables. Large cabbage leaves can be stuffed with savoury fillings, while cabbage preserved in vinegar is a speciality from Alsace-Lorraine. Potatoes are grown widely all over France and potato dishes that originated in France are now popular around the globe. Puréed vegetables dishes, especially those made from pumpkin or root vegetables, and shallots or onions baked in the oven are also typical French accompaniments. Garlic bread and melba toast are served with almost any savoury dish, while croûtons are added to soups, stews and casseroles as a topping.

Garlic bread (serves 6)

> 1 French stick
> 3oz/75g vegan margarine
> 3 garlic cloves, crushed

Cut the French stick into 1 inch/2.5cm diagonal slices. Mix the garlic with the margarine and spread one side of each slice of bread. Re-assemble the stick and wrap in foil. Bake in a preheated oven at 180°C/350°F/Gas mark 4 for 15 minutes. If you prefer the bread crispy, open the foil for the last 5 minutes. Serve hot.

Garlic and herb bread

As for garlic bread, but also add 2 rounded tablespoons of finely chopped fresh herbs of your choice to the margarine.

Croûtons (serves 4)

> 2½ inch/1cm thick slices of bread without crusts
> vegan margarine

Spread one side of each slice of bread with margarine, then cut the slices into small cubes. Put them on a baking tray under a hot grill until golden and crisp. Shake the tray occasionally to ensure even browning.

Garlic croûtons

Add 1 crushed garlic clove to the margarine before spreading and proceed as for croûtons above.

Melba toast (serves 4/6)

4 medium thick slices of wholemeal bread

Toast the bread on both sides, then cut off the crusts. Cut each slice into 4 triangles, then carefully slice each triangle through the middle to make 2 thin triangles. Put these untoasted side up under a hot grill until golden brown. Allow to cool before serving.

Lyonnaise potatoes (serves 4)

1½lb/675g potatoes, peeled and thinly sliced
8oz/225g onions, peeled and finely chopped
1 tablespoon olive oil
black pepper
vegan margarine
chopped fresh parsley

Put the potatoes in a pan and cover with water. Bring to the boil and simmer for 3 minutes, then drain. Fry the onion in the olive oil until soft. Layer the potato and onion in a greased baking dish, seasoning each layer with black pepper. Dot the top with margarine, cover and bake in a preheated oven at 180°C/350°F/Gas mark 4 for 45 minutes. Uncover and bake for a further 5 minutes until browned. Garnish with chopped fresh parsley when serving.

Garlic potatoes (serves 4)

2lb/900g potatoes, peeled and diced
4 garlic cloves, crushed
2 tablespoons olive oil
finely chopped fresh parsley

Boil the potatoes for 3 minutes, drain and dry off on kitchen paper. Heat the oil in a large pan, add the potatoes and fry for 1 minute, stirring until they are coated in oil. Transfer them to a baking dish and bake in a preheated oven at 180°C/350°F/Gas mark 4 for 15 minutes. Add the garlic and stir until well combined. Return to the oven for about 15 minutes, until the potatoes are golden brown. Serve garnished with chopped parsley.

Potato and mushroom bake (serves 4)

> 1½lb/675g potatoes, peeled and diced
> 4oz/100g mushrooms, wiped and chopped
> 2 shallots, peeled and finely chopped
> 2 garlic cloves, crushed
> 1 dessertspoon olive oil
> 4 fl.oz/125ml soya milk
> ½ teaspoon dried thyme
> black pepper
> fresh parsley sprigs

Heat the oil and gently fry the shallots and garlic until softened, then add the mushrooms and cook until the juices begin to run. Boil the potatoes for 3 minutes, drain and add to the mushrooms together with the soya milk and thyme. Season with black pepper and stir well. Bring to the boil and simmer, stirring occasionally, for 5 minutes. Spoon everything into a greased ovenproof dish, cover with foil and bake in a preheated oven at 180°C/350°F/Gas mark 4 for 25 minutes. Use fresh parsley sprigs as garnish when serving.

Creamed herbed potatoes (serves 4)

> 1½lb/675g potatoes, peeled
> 2oz/50g vegan 'cream cheese'

1 rounded tablespoon vegan margarine

6 tablespoons soya milk

1 rounded dessertspoon dried fines herbes, crumbled

black pepper

chopped fresh chives

Cut the potatoes into even-sized chunks and cook them, then drain and dry off over a low heat. Mash the potatoes with the margarine and add the 'cream cheese', soya milk and fines herbes. Season with black pepper and combine thoroughly. Spoon the mixture into a greased ovenproof dish and fork over the top, cover with foil and place in a preheated oven at 180°C/350°F/Gas mark 4 for 10-15 minutes until heated through. Garnish with chopped fresh chives.

Garlic and chervil potato slices (serves 4)

2lb/900g potatoes, peeled

4 garlic cloves, crushed

4 rounded tablespoons finely chopped fresh chervil

1 dessertspoon olive oil

8 fl.oz/225ml soya milk

black pepper

fresh chervil sprigs

Fry the garlic in the oil in a large saucepan. Cut the potatoes into ¼ inch/5mm thick slices and add to the pan together with the chopped chervil and soya milk. Season with black pepper and bring to the boil. Simmer for 10 minutes, stirring occasionally, then transfer to a greased casserole dish. Cover and bake in a preheated oven at 180°C/350°F/Gas mark 4 for 25 minutes. Garnish with fresh chervil sprigs to serve.

Potato, spinach and walnut croquettes (serves 4)

2lb/900g potatoes, peeled

8oz/225g fresh spinach

1oz/25g vegan margarine

black pepper

1½oz/40g breadcrumbs

1oz/25g walnuts, grated

olive oil

Wash the spinach and put it in a pan with only the water that clings to the leaves. Cook until tender, drain and squeeze out excess water and chop the spinach finely. Cut the potatoes into even-sized chunks and cook them. Drain and dry off over a low heat. Mash the potatoes with the margarine, then add the spinach, season with black pepper and combine thoroughly. Mix the breadcrumbs with the walnuts in a small bowl. Take rounded tablespoonfuls of the potato mixture and shape into croquettes. Roll these in the bread-crumbs until completely covered and put them on an oiled baking sheet. Brush with olive oil and bake in a preheated oven at 180°C/350°F/Gas mark 4 for 30 minutes until golden brown.

Red rice with beans (serves 4/6)

8oz/225g red rice

8oz/225g tomatoes, skinned and chopped

8oz/225g red pepper, chopped

8oz/225g cooked haricot beans

2 shallots, peeled and finely chopped

2 garlic cloves, crushed

1 tablespoon olive oil

1 sprig of fresh rosemary

1 sprig of fresh thyme

1 bay leaf

black pepper

24 fl.oz/725ml vegetable stock

chopped fresh parsley

Heat the oil in a large pan and gently fry the red pepper, shallots and garlic for 5 minutes. Add the tomatoes and cook for 2 minutes more. Stir in the rice, rosemary, thyme, bay leaf and stock, season with black pepper and bring to the boil. Cover and simmer for 15 minutes. Add the beans, then continue simmering for another 15 minutes or so until the liquid has been absorbed and the rice is done. Remove the rosemary and thyme sprigs and the bay leaf and spoon the rice into a warmed serving dish. Garnish with fresh chopped parsley before serving.

Garlic and parsley rice (serves 4)

8oz/225g long grain rice

1oz/25g fresh parsley, trimmed and finely chopped

4 garlic cloves, crushed

1 tablespoon olive oil

18 fl.oz/550ml vegetable stock

2 fl.oz/50ml white wine

black pepper

chopped fresh parsley

Heat the oil and gently fry the garlic without browning. Add the rice and stir around for 30 seconds, then the remaining ingredients and combine well. Bring to the boil, cover and simmer gently until the liquid has been absorbed and the rice is cooked. Transfer to a warmed serving dish and garnish with chopped parsley.

Haricot beans in tomato and carrot sauce (serves 4)

8oz/225g cooked haricot beans

14oz/400g tin crushed tomatoes

4oz/100g carrot, scraped and finely chopped

1 onion, peeled and finely chopped

2 garlic cloves, crushed

1 tablespoon olive oil

1 bay leaf

½ teaspoon fennel seed

½ teaspoon tarragon

black pepper

chopped fresh parsley

Fry the carrot, onion and garlic in the oil for 5 minutes. Add the tomatoes, bay leaf, fennel seed and tarragon and season with black pepper. Stir well and bring to the boil, then cover and simmer, stirring occasionally, for 10 minutes. Add the beans and continue simmering for another 5 minutes. Serve garnished with chopped parsley.

Braised carrots with dill (serves 4)

1lb/450g carrots, scraped

1 garlic clove, crushed

1 dessertspoon vegan margarine

1 tablespoon finely chopped fresh dill

3 tablespoons water

black pepper

Halve the carrots lengthwise, then cut them into diagonal slices. Fry the garlic in the margarine in a saucepan, add the carrots, dill and water and season with black pepper. Simmer gently, stirring occasionally, for about 15 minutes until the carrots are just tender.

Green vegetables with garlic crumbs (serves 4)

4oz/100g fresh spinach, shredded

4oz/100g broccoli, chopped

4oz/100g courgette, halved lengthwise and sliced

4oz/100g green beans, topped, tailed and cut into 1 inch/2.5cm lengths

1 onion, peeled and finely chopped

1 garlic clove, crushed

1 tablespoon olive oil

2 tablespoons chopped fresh chives

black pepper

5 fl.oz/150ml vegetable stock

2 fl.oz/50ml soya milk

1 rounded dessertspoon cornflour

topping

1oz/25g breadcrumbs

1 garlic clove, crushed

1 teaspoon vegan margarine

Melt the margarine, add the garlic and breadcrumbs and stir around for 1 minute. Remove from the heat and set aside. Heat the oil and gently fry the onion and garlic until softened. Add the spinach and stir around until it wilts, then add the broccoli, courgette, beans, chives and stock and season with black pepper. Bring to the boil and simmer, stirring occasionally, until the vegetables are just done. Mix the cornflour with the soya milk until smooth, add it to the pan and stir well. Bring to the boil whilst stirring and simmer for a minute or so until the sauce thickens. Transfer to a warmed ovenproof dish and sprinkle the garlic crumbs on top. Place under a hot grill for a couple of minutes to brown.

Petit pois à la française (serves 4)

1lb/450g shelled peas

2oz/50g lettuce, shredded

6 spring onions, trimmed and finely sliced

1 rounded tablespoon vegan margarine

5 tablespoons water

few sprigs of fresh mint

Melt the margarine in a saucepan. Keep a few mint leaves for garnish and put the rest of the sprigs into the pan with the other ingredients. Stir well, cover and cook over a medium heat for 15 minutes, shaking the pan occasionally, until the peas are tender. Remove the mint sprigs before serving garnished with the remaining mint leaves.

Root vegetable gratin (serves 4)

1lb/450g peeled root vegetables (e.g. celeriac, potato, carrot, turnip), grated

7 fl.oz/200ml soya milk

4 spring onions, trimmed and finely chopped

1 rounded tablespoon finely chopped fresh chives

1 teaspoon Dijon mustard

black pepper

topping

1oz/25g breadcrumbs

½oz/15g vegan 'cheese', grated

1 teaspoon parsley

Put the grated vegetables, spring onions, chives, soya milk and mustard in a saucepan, season with black pepper and stir well. Simmer, whilst stirring, for 5 minutes, then transfer to a greased shallow ovenproof dish. Mix the breadcrumbs with the 'cheese' and parsley and sprinkle evenly over the vegetables. Cover with foil and bake in a preheated oven at 180°C/350°F/Gas mark 4 for 15 minutes. Remove the foil and bake for a further 5-10 minutes until golden.

Orange-glazed red cabbage with apple (serves 4)

1lb/450g red cabbage, shredded

1 eating apple, peeled, cored and finely chopped

1oz/25g sultanas

4 fl.oz/125ml fresh orange juice

1 rounded teaspoon arrowroot

1 teaspoon coriander seed, crushed

black pepper

grated orange peel

Put the cabbage and sultanas in a large pan and cover with water. Bring to the boil, cover and simmer for 3 minutes, then drain. Dissolve the arrowroot in the orange juice and pour into a saucepan, then add the coriander seed and season with black pepper. Bring to the boil while stirring, remove from the heat and add the cabbage and sultanas and the apple. Mix well, then spoon into a greased baking dish. Cover with foil and bake in a preheated oven at 180°C/350°F/Gas mark 4 for 25 minutes. Garnish with grated orange peel.

Choucroute (makes 4 1lb/450g jars)

2lb/900g white or red cabbage, finely shredded

2oz/50g salt

pickling vinegar

4 teaspoons black mustard seeds

Layer the cabbage with the salt in a large bowl, cover and leave overnight. Rinse the cabbage thoroughly to remove the salt, drain and pack into sterilised jars together with 1 teaspoonful of black mustard seeds per jar. Cover with pickling vinegar and seal with vinegar-proof tops. Store for at least 10 days before using. Jars of pickled cabbage will keep for up to 3 months if stored in a cool, dark cupboard.

Vegetable julienne sauté (served 4)

> 1½lb/675g peeled root vegetables (a mixture of celeriac, carrot, turnip, potato, kohl rabi), cut into 1 inch/2.5cm julienne strips
>
> 1 tablespoon vegan margarine
>
> 2 garlic cloves, crushed
>
> 2 tablespoons finely chopped fresh chives
>
> black pepper
>
> 4 fl.oz/125ml water

Melt the margarine in a large pan and fry the julienne strips and garlic for 5 minutes. Add the water and half of the chives and season with black pepper. Bring to the boil, cover and simmer for about 15 minutes, shaking the pan occasionally to prevent sticking, until the vegetables are done. Serve garnished with the remaining chives in a warmed dish.

SAUCES AND DRESSINGS

Plainly cooked vegetables can be transformed into special dishes simply by serving them with a sauce or dressing. Sauces can also be used as a base for gratin dishes, by mixing a selection of cooked vegetables, beans and pasta with a sauce, adding a savoury breadcrumb topping and placing under a hot grill until golden brown. Rouille is traditionally spooned into bowls of soup just before serving, but it can be used equally well as a dressing for cooked vegetables or salads. Bottles of herb-flavoured vinegars and oils can be bought from the épicerie, the grocery shop, and they are widely used in salad dressings and marinades.

Sun-dried tomato and basil sauce (serves 4/6)

12oz/350g ripe tomatoes, skinned and chopped

½oz/15g sun-dried tomatoes, finely chopped

3 tablespoons boiling water

1 shallot, peeled and finely chopped

1 garlic clove, crushed

1 tablespoon olive oil

2 rounded tablespoons finely chopped fresh basil

black pepper

Soak the sun-dried tomatoes in the boiling water for 2 hours. Heat the oil in a saucepan and fry the shallot and garlic for 3 minutes, then add the sun-dried tomatoes and remaining liquid and simmer for 2 minutes. Add the remaining ingredients and stir well. Bring to the boil, cover and simmer, stirring occasionally, for 15 minutes. Put in a blender and blend until smooth, then reheat before serving.

Béchamel sauce (serves 4)

10 fl.oz/300ml soya milk

½oz/15g vegan margarine

½oz/15g plain flour

1 shallot, peeled and sliced

½ celery stick, trimmed and sliced

1 bay leaf

2 fresh parsley sprigs

black pepper

Bring the soya milk to the boil with the shallot, celery, bay leaf and parsley. Remove from the heat, cover and leave to infuse for 15 minutes, then strain.

Melt the margarine in a saucepan and gradually add the flour, stirring all the time. Cook for 1 minute whilst stirring. Remove from the heat and add the soya milk, a little at a time, whisking well between additions until fully combined. Season with black pepper and return to the heat. Bring back to the boil while stirring and continue stirring until the sauce thickens.

Mornay sauce (serves 4)

10 fl.oz/300ml soya milk
1oz/25g vegan 'cheese', grated
1 rounded dessertspoon vegan 'Parmesan'
½oz/15g vegan margarine
½oz/15g plain flour
½ teaspoon Dijon mustard
black pepper

Melt the margarine, stir in the flour and cook for 1 minute, then remove from the heat. Dissolve the mustard in the soya milk and add to the pan together with the remaining ingredients. Whisk until smooth, return to the heat and bring to the boil while stirring. Continue stirring until the sauce thickens.

Mushroom and brandy sauce (serves 4)

6oz/175g mushrooms, wiped and chopped
1 shallot, peeled and chopped
1 garlic clove, crushed
1 dessertspoon olive oil
2 tablespoons brandy
6 fl.oz/175ml vegetable stock
1 teaspoon dried thyme
1 rounded dessertspoon arrowroot
black pepper

Fry the mushrooms, shallot and garlic in the oil for 5 minutes, then transfer to a blender with the brandy and thyme. Dissolve the arrowroot in the vegetable stock and add. Season with black pepper and blend until smooth. Pour into a double boiler and bring to the boil while stirring. Remove from the heat once the sauce thickens.

Creamy celery and almond sauce (serves 4)

6oz/175g celery, trimmed and finely chopped

3 spring onions, trimmed and sliced

1oz/25g ground almonds, toasted

1 dessertspoon olive oil

1 rounded teaspoon dried chervil

black pepper

4 fl.oz/125ml water

5 fl.oz/150ml soya milk

¼oz/7g cornflour

Fry the celery and spring onions in the oil for 10 minutes. Add the water and chervil, bring to the boil and simmer for 10 minutes, then transfer to a blender. Dissolve the cornflour in the soya milk and add, together with the ground almonds. Season with black pepper and blend smooth. Transfer to a double boiler and bring to the boil while stirring. Continue stirring until the sauce thickens.

Garlic and parsley sauce (serves 4)

1oz/25g white bread

5 fl.oz/150ml soya milk

2 garlic cloves, crushed

1 dessertspoon olive oil

½oz/15g fresh parsley, chopped

black pepper

Break the bread into pieces and soak in the soya milk for 30 minutes. Fry the garlic in the oil, then add to the soaked bread together with the parsley. Season with black pepper and blend the mixture until smooth. Transfer to a small pan and bring to the boil, stirring continuously for a minute or so until the sauce thickens.

Onion and mustard sauce (serves 4)

6oz/175g onion, peeled and finely chopped

1 rounded dessertspoon vegan margarine

4 fl.oz/125ml water

½ teaspoon vegan vegetable bouillon

10 fl.oz/300ml soya milk

1 rounded tablespoon Dijon mustard

1 rounded tablespoon cornflour

black pepper

Fry the onion in the margarine for 5 minutes. Dissolve the bouillon in the water and add to the pan, bring to the boil, cover and simmer for 5 minutes. Dissolve the cornflour and mustard in the soya milk and add, then season with black pepper and stir well. Bring to the boil and stir continuously until the sauce thickens.

Tomato coulis (serves 4)

8oz/225g ripe tomatoes, skinned and chopped

2 tablespoons water

½ teaspoon sugar

black pepper

Put all ingredients in a small pan and bring to the boil. Cover and simmer, stirring occasionally, for 10 minutes until the tomatoes are pulpy. Sieve the mixture and discard the pips. Stir well and put in the fridge until cold.

Red pepper rouille (serves 4/6)

6oz/175g red pepper
1 garlic clove, chopped
4 rounded tablespoons vegan mayonnaise
½ teaspoon cayenne pepper
black pepper

Grill the pepper until the skin is charred and blistered all over. Allow to cool slightly, then carefully remove the skin, stalk, membranes and seeds. Chop the flesh and blend it with the garlic into a purée. Add the mayonnaise and cayenne pepper and season with black pepper. Mix until well combined.

Herb-flavoured vinegar

fresh herbs of your choice (e.g. basil, rosemary, tarragon, thyme,
    or a combination)
red or white wine vinegar

Lightly bruise the leaves of the herbs to release the flavour, then half-fill a vinegar bottle with them. Fill the bottle with red or white wine vinegar and put the stopper on. Leave to infuse in a cool dark place for 3 weeks, shaking the bottle occasionally, before using.

Herb-flavoured oil

As above, but use olive oil instead of vinegar.

Piquant herb dressing (serves 4)

8 rounded tablespoons chopped fresh herbs (e.g. oregano, thyme, marjoram, parsley)

4 tablespoons olive oil

2 dessertspoons white wine vinegar

1 dessertspoon lemon juice

2 medium gherkins, chopped

1 rounded tablespoon capers

2 garlic cloves, chopped

pinch of ground bay leaves

black pepper

Put all ingredients in a blender and blend smooth.

Tartare sauce (serves 6)

8 rounded tablespoons vegan mayonnaise

2 rounded tablespoons finely chopped fresh parsley

1oz/25g gherkin, finely chopped

½oz/15g capers, finely chopped

black pepper

Mix the ingredients until well combined.

Aïoli (serves 4)

4 rounded tablespoons vegan mayonnaise

2 garlic cloves, crushed

1 dessertspoon lemon juice

Combine all ingredients well.

French dressing

5 tablespoons olive oil

1 tablespoon red wine vinegar

1 dessertspoon lemon juice

1 teaspoon Dijon mustard

1 garlic clove, crushed

black pepper

Mix the ingredients thoroughly.

Walnut vinaigrette

5 tablespoons walnut oil

2 tablespoons white wine vinegar

1 tablespoon lemon juice

½oz/15g walnuts, finely chopped

black pepper

Stir everything together until well combined.

Mustard and tarragon dressing

6 tablespoons olive oil

2 tablespoons white wine vinegar

1 tablespoon lemon juice

1 tablespoon Dijon mustard

1 tablespoon dried tarragon, crumbled

black pepper

Mix all the ingredients well.

SALADS

As well as the more elaborate kind, French cooks are also fond of preparing simple salads consisting of a variety of leaves and these are often served between courses to refresh the palate. A typical salad might be a selection of leaves such as curly endive, rocket, lamb's lettuce, batavia, red oak leaf, chicory, watercress, young spinach and fresh herbs. These are lightly dressed just before serving with either a French or a walnut dressing and chopped walnuts and croûtons are sometimes added for extra 'crunch'.

All salads make ideal accompaniments for main courses, while a selection of salads can be turned into a meal when served with a savoury pastry or home-made bread and pâté.

Roasted pepper and chickpea salad (serves 4)

1lb/450g mixed peppers

8oz/225g cooked chickpeas

1 small red onion, peeled

1 garlic clove, crushed

1 dessertspoon capers, chopped

1 dessertspoon olive oil

1 dessertspoon lemon juice

black pepper

finely chopped fresh chervil

Place the peppers on a baking tray under a hot grill, turning occasionally, until the skins blister. When cooled slightly carefully remove the skins, stalks, membranes and seeds and chop the flesh. Put the peppers in a mixing bowl with the chickpeas. Cut a few rings from the onion and keep for garnish, then finely chop the rest of the onion and add it to the bowl with the garlic and capers. Mix the olive oil with the lemon juice and spoon over the salad. Season with black pepper and toss thoroughly. Transfer to a serving bowl, arrange the onion rings on top and garnish with fresh chervil.

Grated carrot and sesame seed salad (serves 4)

1lb/450g carrots, scraped and grated

1 garlic clove, crushed

½oz/15g sesame seeds, toasted

2 tablespoons olive oil

1 tablespoon white wine vinegar

1 dessertspoon lemon juice

black pepper

finely shredded crisp lettuce

Mix the olive oil with the garlic, vinegar and lemon juice. Put the carrots and sesame seeds in a large bowl and add the dressing, then season with black pepper and toss well. Arrange some shredded lettuce on a serving plate and pile the salad on top.

Grilled tomato and garlic croûton salad (serves 4)

8oz/225g cherry tomatoes, skinned and halved

2½ inch/1cm thick slices of bread without crusts

1 rounded dessertspoon vegan margarine

1 garlic clove, crushed

1 small red onion, peeled and finely chopped

2 rounded tablespoons finely chopped fresh parsley

olive oil

black pepper

Mix the garlic with the margarine and spread it on one side of each slice of bread. Cut the bread into cubes and place them on a baking tray under a hot grill. Toast the cubes until golden, shaking the tray occasionally to ensure even browning. Brush the tomatoes with olive oil and put them under a hot grill until they begin to soften. Transfer them to a mixing bowl and add the croûtons, onion and half of the parsley, season with black pepper and toss thoroughly. Serve garnished with the remaining parsley.

Warm potato and walnut salad (serves 4)

1½lb/675g new potatoes, scraped

1oz/25g walnuts, chopped

4 spring onions, trimmed and finely sliced

2 tablespoons vegan mayonnaise

1 tablespoon Dijon mustard

1 tablespoon lemon juice

black pepper

chopped fresh chives

Steam the potatoes. Meanwhile, mix the mayonnaise with the mustard and lemon juice. Dice the cooked potatoes and place them in a mixing bowl. Spoon the dressing over the potatoes and mix, then add the walnuts and spring onions and season with black pepper. Toss well, spoon into a serving bowl and garnish with chopped chives.

Beetroot and sultana salad (serves 4)

12oz/350g raw beetroot, peeled and grated

1oz/25g sultanas

2 tablespoons fresh orange juice

1 dessertspoon olive oil

1 teaspoon red wine vinegar

black pepper

finely grated orange peel

Put the beetroot, sultanas and orange juice in a saucepan and cook over a medium heat for 5 minutes, stirring regularly. Mix the olive oil with the vinegar and add. Season with black pepper and toss well. Put the salad in a serving bowl, cover and refrigerate until cold. Garnish with finely grated orange peel when serving.

Mixed bean salad (serves 4)

8oz/225g French beans, topped, tailed and cut into ½ inch/1cm diagonal slices

8oz/225g cooked mixed beans (e.g. haricot, flageolet, red kidney)

2oz/50g cucumber, finely chopped

4 spring onions, trimmed and finely sliced

1 celery stick, trimmed and finely sliced

1 garlic clove, crushed

2 tablespoons finely chopped fresh chives

1 tablespoon finely chopped fresh tarragon

1 rounded teaspoon Dijon mustard

1 tablespoon olive oil

2 dessertspoons white wine vinegar

black pepper

finely shredded chicory leaves

Steam the French beans until just tender, then rinse under cold water. Drain well and put them in a bowl with the mixed beans, cucumber, spring onions, celery, garlic, chives and tarragon. Mix the mustard with the olive oil and vinegar, season with black pepper and add to the salad. Toss thoroughly. Arrange some shredded chicory leaves on a serving plate and pile the salad on top.

Red rice salad (serves 4)

4oz/100g red rice

3oz/75g shelled peas

3oz/75g sweetcorn kernels

3oz/75g red pepper, finely chopped

4 cherry tomatoes, quartered

1 small red onion

1 celery stick, trimmed and finely chopped

1 rounded tablespoon capers, chopped

1 garlic clove, crushed

1 rounded tablespoon finely chopped fresh thyme

1 rounded tablespoon finely chopped fresh parsley

1 tablespoon olive oil

1 dessertspoon red wine vinegar

black pepper

Cook the rice, drain and rinse under cold running water. Drain well and put in a mixing bowl. Blanch the peas and sweetcorn, then drain and rinse under cold water. Add to the rice with the red pepper, tomatoes, celery, capers and herbs. Keep a few rings from the onion, finely chop the rest and add to the salad. Mix the olive oil with the vinegar and garlic, spoon this dressing over the salad and season with black pepper. Toss well and transfer the salad to a serving dish. Cover and chill for a couple of hours. Garnish with the onion rings before serving.

Celeriac rémoulade (serves 4)

> 1lb/450g peeled celeriac, grated
> 4 rounded tablespoons vegan mayonnaise
> 1 rounded tablespoon Dijon mustard
> 2 rounded tablespoons chopped fresh chervil
> 1 dessertspoon lemon juice
> black pepper
> squeeze of lemon juice
> shredded crisp lettuce leaves
> fresh chervil leaves

Put the celeriac in a pan and cover with water, add a squeeze of lemon juice and bring to the boil. Simmer for 1 minute, then drain and rinse under cold running water. Drain well and put in a bowl. Mix the mayonnaise with the mustard, chopped chervil and lemon juice. Season with black pepper, spoon over the celeriac and toss. Arrange some shredded lettuce on a serving plate and pile the rémoulade on top. Garnish with chervil leaves to serve.

Artichoke rémoulade

Follow the recipe for celeriac rémoulade above, but use 1lb/450g peeled Jerusalem artichokes instead of celeriac.

Mangetout and leek vinaigrette (serves 4)

8oz/225g leek, trimmed

8oz/225g mangetout, topped and tailed

2 tablespoons olive oil

1 dessertspoon lemon juice

½ teaspoon Dijon mustard

black pepper

1 tablespoons finely grated lemon peel

2 rounded tablespoons finely chopped fresh parsley

shredded crisp lettuce leaves

Cut the leeks in half lengthwise, then into ½ inch/1cm slices. Cut the mangetout into ½ inch/1cm diagonal slices. Steam the leek and mangetout separately until just tender and put them in a bowl. Mix the olive oil with the lemon juice and mustard and spoon over the hot vegetables, add the lemon peel and parsley, season with black pepper and toss well. Cover and keep in the fridge until cold. Arrange some shredded lettuce on a serving plate and pile the salad on top.

Aubergine and lentil salad (serves 4)

8oz/225g aubergine, diced

1 red onion, peeled and finely chopped

6oz/175g tomato, skinned and chopped

3oz/75g puy lentils

3 tablespoons olive oil

2 rounded tablespoons finely chopped mixed fresh herbs

1 garlic clove, crushed

1 teaspoon red wine vinegar

black pepper

Cook the lentils, drain them and rinse them under cold running water. Fry the aubergine and onion in 2 tablespoonfuls of the oil for about 15 minutes, stirring frequently, until done. Put in a mixing bowl with the lentils, tomato, herbs and garlic. Mix the remaining oil with the vinegar and add to the salad. Season with black pepper and mix thoroughly. Spoon into a serving bowl, cover and chill.

Mushroom and garlic salad (serves 4)

1lb/450g button mushrooms, wiped and halved

4 garlic cloves, crushed

2 dessertspoons olive oil

4 tablespoons finely chopped fresh parsley

black pepper

chopped walnuts

curly lettuce leaves

Fry the mushrooms and garlic in the oil for a couple of minutes until the juices begin to run. Transfer to a bowl, cover and refrigerate until cold. Add the parsley and season with black pepper. Mix well, then arrange some curly lettuce leaves on a serving plate, pile the salad on top and garnish with chopped walnuts.

DESSERTS

An abundance of fruit is grown in all areas of France and many are preserved by bottling or drying for use in the winter months. There are thousands of acres of orchards and dozens of varieties of apples and pears are grown for the home market and for export. Fresh fruit salads made from regionally produced, seasonal fruits such as melons, cherries, nectarines, strawberries, apricots, grapes and greengages make a refreshing dessert and a dash of fruit-flavoured liqueur is often added to the syrup. Open and closed pastry tarts filled with fresh or dried fruits and cooked vol-au-vent cases stuffed with fruit and nut fillings are also traditional favourites.

Iced apricot and almond cream with dried fruit compote (serves 4)

cream

2oz/50g dried apricots, finely chopped

4 fl.oz/125ml water

1oz/25g ground almonds, toasted

9 fl.oz/250ml carton soya 'cream'

1 tablespoon brandy

compote

8oz/225g dried fruit (e.g. a mixture of prunes, apples, pears, peaches, figs), finely chopped

7 fl.oz/200ml fresh apple juice

2 inch/5cm stick of cinnamon

garnish

toasted flaked almonds

Put the apricots and water in a small saucepan and bring to the boil. Cover and simmer for about 20 minutes until the liquid has been absorbed and the apricots are soft. Allow to cool slightly, then blend until smooth with the ground almonds, 'cream' and brandy. Spoon the mixture into four 3 inch/8cm diameter ramekin dishes. Cover and freeze for about 5 hours until just solid.

Bring the dried fruit to the boil with the apple juice and cinnamon stick, cover and simmer for about 20 minutes, stirring occasionally, until the juice has been absorbed. Remove the cinnamon stick, transfer the fruit to a covered container and keep in the fridge until cold.

Run a sharp knife round the edges of the dishes and turn the iced creams out onto serving plates. If the cream has become too hard, keep it at room temperature for 30 minutes before serving. Spoon the fruit compote over the top and garnish with flaked almonds.

Autumn fruit gelée (serves 4)

8oz/225g eating apple, peeled, cored and chopped

8oz/225g dessert pear, peeled, cored and chopped

5oz/150g blackberries

1oz/25g demerara sugar

8 fl.oz/225ml fresh apple juice

1 rounded dessertspoon arrowroot

10 fl.oz/300ml fruit-flavoured soya yoghurt

Keep 1oz/25g of blackberries for garnish and put the rest in a saucepan with the apple, pear, sugar and apple juice. Bring to the boil and simmer until the fruit is cooked. Strain the juice into a small pan and divide the fruit between 4 serving glasses. Mix the arrowroot with the juice until smooth. Bring to the boil whilst stirring, then spoon the mixture over the fruit in the glasses. Cover and refrigerate for a few hours until set. Top with yoghurt and the remaining blackberries just before serving.

Spiced plum clafoutis (serves 4/6)

12oz/350g plums, stoned and chopped

batter

10 fl.oz/300ml soya milk

3½oz/90g fine wholemeal self raising flour

½oz/15g soya flour

1½oz/40g demerara sugar

¼ teaspoon ground mixed spice

topping

1 rounded dessertspoon demerara sugar

¼ teaspoon ground mixed spice

Whisk the batter ingredients until smooth, then leave to stand for 30 minutes.

Spread the plums over the base of a greased 9 inch/23cm round flan dish. Whisk the batter again and pour over the plums. Mix the sugar and spice for the topping and sprinkle evenly over the top. Bake in a preheated oven at 180°C/350°F/Gas mark 4 for about 35 minutes until golden. Serve hot with yoghurt or ice cream.

Chocolate and hazelnut ramekins (serves 4)

16 fl.oz/475ml soya milk

1½oz/40g demerara sugar

1oz/25g cornflour

¾oz/20g cocoa powder

¾oz/20g hazelnuts, finely chopped and toasted

½oz/15g vegan chocolate, grated

Mix the cocoa powder, cornflour and sugar with the soya milk until smooth. Pour into a double boiler, bring to the boil while stirring and continue stirring for a minute or two until the sauce thickens. Pour into four 3 inch/8cm ramekin dishes, cover and put in the fridge until set. Mix the chopped hazelnuts with the grated chocolate and sprinkle on top before serving.

Melon and champagne sorbet (serves 4/6)

1lb/450g ripe charentais melon flesh, chopped

8 fl.oz/225ml champagne

1oz/25g sugar

Put the melon in a blender with the champagne and sugar and blend until smooth. Pour into a shallow lidded freezerproof container and freeze for 1 hour. Whisk well and return to the freezer for about 5 hours until frozen. Keep at room temperature for 30 minutes before serving if the sorbet has become too solid.

Tarte tatin (serves 4)

base

4oz/100g fine wholemeal self raising flour

2oz/50g vegan margarine

1oz/25g walnuts, grated

½ oz/15g demerara sugar

½ oz/15g soya flour

3 tablespoons soya milk

topping

1 eating apple, peeled, cored and chopped

1 dessert pear, peeled, cored and chopped

2 large plums, stoned and chopped

½oz/15g vegan margarine

½oz/15g demerara sugar

¼ teaspoon ground cinnamon

chopped walnuts

First make the topping. Gently heat the margarine, sugar and cinnamon in a large saucepan until melted. Add the fruit and stir until coated, then spoon it into a greased 7 inch/18cm deep tart tin.

Put the wholemeal flour in a mixing bowl, rub in the margarine and stir in the walnuts and sugar. Mix the soya flour with the soya milk until smooth and add to the bowl. Mix well until a soft dough forms. Turn out onto a floured board and roll out into a 7 inch/18cm circle. Carefully place the dough on top of the fruit and press it down evenly. Bake in a preheated oven at 180°C/350°F/Gas mark 4 for about 30 minutes until golden brown. Run a knife around the edges to loosen, then invert the tarte onto a serving dish. Garnish with chopped walnuts and serve hot with yoghurt or ice cream.

Pears poached in red wine (serves 4)

4 dessert pears, peeled

6 fl.oz/175ml red wine

6 fl.oz/175ml fresh orange juice

2 tablespoons demerara sugar

2 inch/5cm stick of cinnamon

8 cloves

finely grated orange peel

Bring the wine, orange juice, sugar, cinnamon and cloves to the boil. Add the pears and simmer, basting with the liquid and turning occasionally, for about 15 minutes until the pears are just tender. Remove the pears with a slotted spoon and put them in 4 serving bowls. Strain the remaining liquid to remove the spices, then boil it rapidly for a minute or two until it reduces and thickens. Spoon this syrup over the pears. Cover the bowls and keep them in the fridge until cold. Serve topped with yoghurt and garnished with grated orange peel.

Chocolate, pear and almond tart (serves 6)

pastry

4½oz/115g fine wholemeal self raising flour

¼oz/7g cocoa powder

2oz/50g vegan margarine

water

filling

8oz/225g dessert pears, peeled, cored and sliced

3oz/75g fine wholemeal self raising flour

1oz/25g ground almonds

1oz/25g vegan margarine

1oz/25g demerara sugar

¼oz/7g cocoa powder

4 fl.oz/125ml soya milk

topping

1oz/25g vegan chocolate, broken

toasted flaked almonds

Sift the flour and cocoa powder for the pastry into a mixing bowl, rub in the margarine and add enough water to make a soft dough. Turn out onto a floured board and roll out to fit a greased 7 inch/18cm diameter loose-bottomed flan tin. Prick the base and bake blind in a preheated oven at 180°C/350°F/Gas mark 4 for 5 minutes.

Heat the margarine and sugar for the filling until melted. Remove from the heat and add the ground almonds, then add the sifted flour and cocoa powder and the soya milk alternately, mixing well between additions. Arrange the pear slices in the flan case and spoon this sponge mixture evenly over them. Return to the oven for 30 minutes until springy to the touch in the centre.

Melt the chocolate in a bowl over a pan of boiling water and drizzle it over the tart. Scatter some toasted flaked almonds on top, cut into wedges and serve warm with ice cream or yoghurt.

Apple ice cream with blackberry coulis (serves 4)

ice cream

8oz/225g eating apples, peeled, cored and chopped

9 fl.oz/250ml carton vegan 'cream'

1 teaspoon lemon juice

1 dessertspoon sugar

coulis

12oz/350g blackberries

1 rounded tablespoon sugar

1 dessertspoon water

Put the apple, lemon juice and sugar in a pan and cook gently until the apple is soft. Mash the apple smooth and mix with the 'cream' until well combined. Transfer to a shallow lidded freezerproof container and freeze for 2 hours. Whisk the mixture, then return it to the freezer for a few hours until frozen. If it has frozen too solidly it will need to be kept at room temperature for 30 minutes before serving.

Keep 8 blackberries for garnish and put the rest in a saucepan with the sugar and water. Cook over a gentle heat for a few minutes until the fruit softens, then press it through a sieve and discard the pips. Stir the purée and refrigerate until cold.

Scoop the ice cream into 4 serving bowls and spoon the blackberry coulis over the top. Garnish with the remaining blackberries.

Pear ice cream with raspberry coulis

Follow the apple ice cream recipe above, but use 8oz/225g dessert pears instead of the apples and 12oz/350g raspberries instead of the blackberries.

Greengage and walnut charlotte (serves 4)

4oz/100g breadcrumbs
1oz/25g walnuts, finely chopped
¾oz/20g vegan margarine
1½oz/40g demerara sugar
¼ teaspoon ground cloves
1lb/450g greengages, stoned and chopped

Put the greengages in a pan with 1oz/25g of the sugar and cook gently until they are just soft. Melt the margarine, then add the breadcrumbs, walnuts, ground cloves and remaining sugar and stir around over a medium heat for a couple of minutes. Spoon half of the fruit into an 8 inch/20cm diameter baking dish and top with half of the breadcrumb mixture. Repeat these layers and press down firmly and evenly. Cover with foil and bake in a preheated oven at 180°C/350°F/Gas mark 4 for 20 minutes. Remove the foil and bake for another 10 minutes until golden and crispy on top. Serve hot with yoghurt or ice cream.

Nectarine custard cups (serves 4)

1lb/450g nectarines, stoned and chopped

10 fl.oz/300ml soya milk

1oz/25g sugar

1oz/25g cornflour

1 teaspoon vanilla essence

1 nectarine, stoned and sliced

toasted flaked almonds

Put the chopped nectarines in a saucepan with the sugar and cook gently until the nectarines are soft. Mix the cornflour with the soya milk until smooth, then pour into a blender with the cooked nectarines and the vanilla essence. Blend smooth and put in a double boiler. Bring to the boil while stirring and continue stirring for a minute or so until the custard thickens, then divide it between 4 sundae glasses. Cover and chill until set. Before serving arrange a couple of slices of nectarine on top of each custard and garnish with toasted flaked almonds.

Orange and apricot crêpes (serves 4)

crêpes

4oz/100g plain flour

1oz/25g soya flour

12 fl.oz/350ml soya milk

½ teaspoon ground cinnamon

vegan margarine

sauce

6 fl.oz/175ml fresh orange juice

2 fl.oz/50ml orange-flavoured liqueur

1 rounded tablespoon finely grated orange peel

1 tablespoon demerara sugar

1 dessertspoon vegan margarine

1 rounded teaspoon arrowroot

topping

4oz/100g dried apricots

5 fl.oz/150ml fresh orange juice

4 fl.oz/125ml plain soya yoghurt

Put the apricots and orange juice into a small pan and bring to the boil. Cover and simmer until the liquid has been absorbed and the apricots are tender. Mash them smooth, then mix with the yoghurt and chill for a few hours.

Whisk the plain and soya flours and the cinnamon with the soya milk until smooth. Cover and chill for 2 hours. Whisk the batter again, then melt a little margarine in an 8 inch/20cm non-stick frying pan and make 8 pancakes. Fold each pancake in half and then in half again. Keep them warm while making the sauce.

Dissolve the arrowroot in the orange juice and pour into a large frying pan with the remaining sauce ingredients. Heat gently until the margarine melts and the sugar dissolves. Add the folded pancakes and cook for about 1 minute on each side. Put 2 crêpes on each serving dish and top with the apricot and orange yoghurt.

Apple bourdelots (serves 4)

4 eating apples, peeled and cored

soya milk

soya yoghurt

pastry

6oz/175g fine wholemeal self raising flour

2oz/50g vegan margarine

water

filling

1oz/25g raisins

1oz/25g sultanas

2 tablespoons apple juice

1 tablespoon demerara sugar

½oz/15g walnuts, finely chopped

¼ teaspoon ground cloves

Mix the raisins, sultanas, apple juice, sugar and ground cloves in a bowl, cover and leave to soak for 2 hours.

Rub the margarine into the flour and add enough water to bind. Knead the pastry well and divide into 4 equal pieces. Roll each piece out on a floured board into a circle of about 5½ inches/14cm. Add the walnuts to the filling and mix well. Fill the hollows of the apples with the filling mixture, pressing it down firmly. Place a filled apple on each pastry circle and pull the pastry up towards the top of the apple to enclose it. Squeeze the pastry gently round each apple to neaten. Put them in a greased baking dish and brush all over with soya milk. Bake in a preheated oven at 180°C/350°F/Gas mark 4 for 30-35 minutes until golden brown. Serve hot, topped with yoghurt.

BREADS

Bread is usually bought fresh each day from the local boulangerie, the bakery, where an amazing range of sweet and savoury breads are baked on the premises at least twice a day. All kinds of grains are ground and used in breadmaking and Paris is often referred to as the breadbasket of France because of the quantity of cereals grown in the surrounding countryside. Some sort of bread is eaten with every meal and stale bread is made into breadcrumbs or croûtons or blended in sauces. Home-made breads are best eaten warm on the day of baking. To store, cut the breads into slices, wrap in foil and freeze, and when needed allow the bread to thaw, then put it, wrapped in foil, in a moderate oven for about 10 minutes until heated through.

Walnut bread

6oz/175g plain flour

6oz/175g plain wholemeal flour

2oz/50g walnuts, finely chopped

2oz/50g vegan margarine

½ sachet easy-blend yeast

½ teaspoon salt

approx. 6 fl.oz/175ml soya milk, warmed

extra soya milk

Sift the two flours and salt into a mixing bowl and rub in the margarine. Stir in the yeast and walnuts, then gradually add the warmed soya milk until a soft dough forms. Knead the dough well, return it to the bowl, cover and leave in a warm place for 30 minutes until risen. Knead the dough again, then shape it into a ball and put it on a greased baking sheet. Cut a cross in the top with a sharp knife and keep it in a warm place for 1 hour to rise again. Brush with soya milk and bake in a preheated oven at 180°C/350°F/Gas mark 4 for 20-25 minutes until golden brown. Transfer to a wire rack and allow to cool slightly before cutting into slices.

Maizemeal, onion and oregano bread

1lb/450g plain flour

8oz/225g maizemeal

8oz/225g onion, peeled and finely chopped

1 sachet easy-blend yeast

1 teaspoon salt

2 tablespoons olive oil

1 rounded tablespoon dried oregano

approx. 12 fl.oz/350ml warm water

extra olive oil

onion seeds

Heat one tablespoonful of oil and gently fry the onion until soft. Mix the flour, maizemeal, yeast, salt and oregano in a large bowl. Stir in the onion and the other tablespoonful of oil and gradually add the water until a soft dough forms. Turn out onto a floured board and knead well. Return to the bowl, cover and leave to rise for 1 hour in a warm place. Knead the dough again, then shape into an oval and place on a greased baking sheet. Make a few slits in the top and put in a warm place for another 30 minutes. Lightly brush the top with olive oil and sprinkle with onion seeds. Bake in a preheated oven at 200°C/400°F/Gas mark 6 for 20-25 minutes until golden. Slide onto a wire rack and cut into slices once the bread has cooled slightly.

Baguette

> 12oz/350g plain flour
> ½ sachet easy-blend yeast
> ½ teaspoon salt
> 1oz/25g vegan margarine, melted
> approx. 6 fl.oz/175ml warm water
> sesame seeds
> *glaze*
> ½ teaspoon salt
> 1 dessertspoon boiling water

Put the flour, salt and yeast in a bowl and mix. Add the melted margarine and stir well, then gradually add the warm water until a soft dough forms. Knead the dough thoroughly, return it to the bowl, cover and leave in a warm place for an hour. Turn the dough out onto a floured board and knead again, then divide it into 2 equal pieces and roll each one into an 11 inch/28cm 'sausage' shape. Place them on a greased baking sheet and make a few slits in the tops with a sharp knife. Allow to rise in a warm place for 30 minutes. Dissolve the salt for the glaze in the boiling water and brush all over the dough. Sprinkle sesame seeds on top.

Fill a baking dish three-quarters full with boiling water and place on the bottom shelf of a preheated oven at 200°C/400°F/Gas mark 6 to create steam in the oven. Put the baguettes on the top shelf and bake for 20-25 minutes until browned. Allow to cool a little, then cut into slices to serve.

Olive and thyme flatbread

8oz/225g plain flour

½ sachet easy-blend yeast

½ teaspoon salt

1oz/25g green olives, chopped

2 tablespoons olive oil

2 rounded teaspoons dried thyme

approx. 4 fl.oz/125ml warm water

8 green olives, halved

extra olive oil

Put the flour, yeast and salt in a large bowl, add the chopped olives, olive oil and thyme and mix well. Gradually add the water until a soft dough forms. Knead the dough, then shape into a flat round 8 inches/20cm in diameter. Transfer to a greased baking sheet and leave for 1 hour in a warm place until risen. Brush the round with olive oil and press the olive halves into the top of the dough. Bake in a preheated oven at 200°C/400°F/Gas mark 6 for about 15 minutes until golden brown. Cut into wedges and serve warm.

Seeded twist

12oz/350g plain wholemeal flour

1oz/25g sunflower seeds

½oz/15g linseed

½oz/15g sesame seeds

2 tablespoons olive oil

½ sachet easy-blend yeast

½ teaspoon salt

approx. 7 fl.oz/200ml warm water

soya milk

extra seeds

Mix the flour, sunflower seeds, linseed, sesame seeds, salt and yeast in a large bowl. Add the oil and combine well, then gradually add the water until a soft dough forms. Knead the dough thoroughly, return it to the bowl, cover and leave to rise for an hour in a warm place. Knead the dough again and divide it into 2 equal portions. Roll each piece into a 'sausage' shape 12 inches/30cm long. Twist the two shapes together and compress slightly so that they stick together. Place on a greased baking sheet and leave in a warm place for 30 minutes. Brush the top with soya milk and sprinkle with seeds. Bake in a preheated oven at 200°C/400°F/Gas mark 6 for 15-20 minutes until golden. Allow to cool on a wire rack before cutting into slices.

Pumpkin bread

1lb/450g plain flour

8oz/225g pumpkin flesh, grated

2 tablespoons olive oil

½ sachet easy-blend yeast

½ teaspoon salt

½ teaspoon paprika

Put the pumpkin in a saucepan and cover with water. Bring to the boil and simmer for 30 seconds, then drain over a bowl and keep the cooking liquid. Mix the flour with the yeast, salt and paprika and stir in the pumpkin and olive oil. Gradually add enough of the cooking liquid for the mixture to bind together. Turn the dough out onto a floured board and knead well. Shape it to fit a base-lined and greased 9 inch/23cm loaf tin. Cover and leave in a warm place for 1 hour to rise. Bake in a preheated oven at 200°C/400°F/Gas mark 6 for 30 minutes until golden brown. Leave in the tin for 15 minutes, then turn out onto a wire rack and allow to cool further before cutting into slices.

Nutty buckwheat and raisin bread

8oz/225g plain flour

4oz/100g buckwheat flour

2oz/50g mixed nuts, finely chopped

2oz/50g raisins, chopped

2 tablespoons fresh apple juice

2oz/50g vegan margarine, melted

½ sachet easy-blend yeast

½ teaspoon salt

approx. 4½ fl.oz/135ml warm water

soya milk

Soak the raisins in the apple juice for an hour. Put the plain and buckwheat flours in a mixing bowl with the salt and yeast. Mix well, then stir in the soaked raisins and any remaining juice. Keep 1 tablespoonful of the chopped nuts and add the rest to the bowl together with the margarine. Combine well, then gradually add the water until a soft dough forms. Turn out onto a floured board and knead thoroughly. Shape the dough into a fat oval and put this on a greased baking sheet. Brush the top with soya milk and sprinkle the remaining nuts on top. Press these in lightly, then leave in a warm place for an hour and 30 minutes until risen. Bake in a preheated oven at 200°C/400°F/Gas mark 6 for about 20 minutes until golden. Transfer to a wire rack to cool before cutting into slices.

Petits pains au chocolat (makes 8)

12oz/350g plain flour

1½oz/40g vegan margarine, melted

1½oz/40g demerara sugar

½oz/15g cocoa powder

½oz/15g vegan chocolate, grated

½ sachet easy-blend yeast

approx. 6 fl.oz/175ml soya milk, warmed

1 dessertspoon vegan margarine, melted

Sift the flour and cocoa powder into a large bowl. Stir in the yeast and sugar, add the 1½oz/40g melted margarine and mix well. Add the grated chocolate, then gradually the soya milk until a soft dough forms. Knead the dough well and return it to the bowl. Cover and leave to rise for an hour in a warm place. Knead the dough again and divide it into 8 equal pieces. Form each piece into a small oval and put them on a greased baking sheet. Make a lengthwise slit in the top of each roll and leave in a warm place for another 30 minutes. Lightly brush the remaining melted margarine over the rolls and bake them in a preheated oven at 200°C/400°F/Gas mark 6 for 15 minutes. Put the rolls on a wire rack to cool slightly before serving.

BAKING

France is famed for its cake shops, where a vast range of cakes and sweet and savoury pastries are made on the premises and beautifully displayed in the shop window. Some pâtisseries also include a café and these are very popular places to meet up with friends for coffee and cakes. Luckily, many of the cakes can be authentically reproduced simply by using vegan alternatives to dairy products. The cakes below all freeze well.

Apple and almond slices (makes 8)

8oz/225g eating apple, peeled and finely chopped

6oz/175g fine wholemeal self raising flour

2oz/50g ground almonds

2oz/50g vegan margarine

2oz/50g demerara sugar

½oz/15g soya flour

5 fl.oz/150ml fresh apple juice

½ teaspoon almond essence

½oz/15g flaked almonds, chopped

Cream the margarine with the sugar and almond essence, add the ground almonds and apple and mix thoroughly. Combine the soya flour with the apple juice and add, alternating with the flour. Stir very well, then spoon the mixture into a lined and greased 7 inch/18cm square baking tin. Press down evenly and sprinkle the chopped almonds on top, pressing them in lightly with the back of a spoon. Cover with foil and bake in a preheated oven at 180°C/350°F/Gas mark 4 for 35 minutes. Remove the foil and return to the oven for about 10 minutes until golden. Allow to cool in the tin for 10 minutes, then transfer to a wire rack to cool completely before cutting into 8 equal slices.

Hazelnut biscuits (makes about 20)

4oz/100g plain flour

2oz/50g vegan margarine

1½oz/40g demerara sugar

1oz/25g hazelnuts, finely grated and toasted

1 rounded teaspoon baking powder

1 tablespoon soya milk

10 hazelnuts, halved

Cream the margarine with the sugar in a large bowl. Add the grated hazelnuts and combine well. Work in the sifted flour and baking powder, then add the soya milk and mix until everything binds together. Take heaped teaspoonfuls of the mixture and roll into balls in the palm of the hand. Flatten each ball slightly and put them on a greased baking tray. Press a hazelnut half into the top of each biscuit and bake them in a preheated oven at 180°C/350°F/Gas mark 4 for about 12 minutes until golden brown. Carefully slide onto a wire rack and allow to cool.

Chocolate, cherry and walnut gâteau

8oz/225g fine wholemeal self raising flour

4oz/100g glacé cherries, washed, dried and quartered

2oz/50g walnuts, grated

1oz/25g demerara sugar

½oz/15g cocoa powder

1 rounded tablespoon golden syrup

1 rounded tablespoon sugar-free cherry jam

7 fl.oz/200ml soya milk

5 fl.oz/150ml sunflower oil

filling

sugar-free cherry jam

topping

3oz/75g vegan chocolate, broken

glacé cherry halves

walnut halves

Combine the sunflower oil, golden syrup, jam, sugar and walnuts in a large bowl. Stir in the cherries, then add the soya milk and the sifted flour and cocoa powder alternately, mixing well between additions. Divide the mixture equally between 2 lined and greased 7 inch/18cm diameter sponge tins, spreading it out evenly. Bake in a preheated oven at 170°C/325°F/Gas mark 3 for about 20 minutes until the sponges are springy to the touch in the centre. Carefully turn them out onto a wire rack.

Once cooled, spread one of the sponges with a layer of cherry jam and place the other sponge on top. Melt the chocolate in a bowl over a pan of boiling water and spread it evenly over the top and sides of the cake. Arrange some glacé cherry and walnut halves on the top, then cover and refrigerate for a few hours for the chocolate to set.

Upside-down pear and hazelnut cake

8oz/225g firm dessert pears, peeled, cored and sliced

1 dessertspoon golden syrup

6oz/175g fine wholemeal self raising flour

3oz/75g hazelnuts, toasted

3oz/75g vegan margarine

2oz/50g demerara sugar

1oz/25g soya flour

8 fl.oz/225ml soya milk

Chop a tablespoonful of hazelnuts for decoration and grate the remaining nuts. Cream the margarine with the sugar. Whisk the soya flour with the soya milk and add to the bowl, alternating with the grated nuts and the flour, and mix well. Base-line and grease a 7 inch/18cm round cake tin. Warm the golden syrup and spoon it evenly into the tin. Arrange the pear slices in a circular pattern in the base and spoon the cake mixture on top, pressing it down evenly to fill any spaces between the pears. Bake in a preheated oven at 180°C/350°F/Gas mark 4 for 30-35 minutes until golden and firm in the centre. Run a sharp knife around the edges of the tin to loosen and invert the cake onto a wire rack. Carefully remove the lining paper and scatter the chopped hazelnuts on the top.

Apricot frangipane (serves 8)

base

4oz/100g fine wholemeal self raising flour

1½oz/40g vegan margarine

soya milk

filling

4oz/100g dried apricots, finely chopped

4 fl.oz/125ml water

topping

3oz/75g fine wholemeal self raising flour

2oz/50g ground almonds

2oz/50g vegan margarine

1oz/25g demerara sugar

½oz/15g soya flour

5 fl.oz/150ml soya milk

1 teaspoon almond essence

2 rounded tablespoons sugar-free apricot jam

1 rounded tablespoon flaked almonds, toasted and chopped

Put the apricots and water in a small saucepan and bring to the boil. Cover and simmer gently until the liquid has been absorbed and the apricots are soft, then remove from the heat and mash the apricots.

Make the base by rubbing the margarine into the flour. Add enough soya milk to make a soft dough, then turn out onto a floured board and roll out to fit the base of a greased 13 x 4 inch/33 x 10cm loose-bottomed flan tin. Prick the base with a fork and bake blind in a preheated oven at 180°C/350°F/Gas mark 4 for 5 minutes.

To make the topping cream the margarine with the sugar and almond essence, then stir in the ground almonds. Whisk the soya flour with the milk and add alternately with the flour, mixing thoroughly. Spoon the mashed apricots evenly over the base and spread the topping over the apricots. Return to the oven for about 35 minutes until golden brown.

Heat the apricot jam in a small pan until runny, then brush evenly over the top. Sprinkle with the flaked almonds and allow to cool before cutting into slices.

Almond sables (makes approx. 25)

4oz/100g plain flour

2oz/50g ground almonds

2oz/50g vegan margarine

1½oz/40g demerara sugar

1 rounded teaspoon baking powder

1 teaspoon almond essence

approx. 2 tablespoons soya milk

Sift the flour and baking powder into a mixing bowl and stir in the ground almonds. Rub in the margarine, then stir in the sugar. Add the almond essence and gradually the soya milk, until a soft dough forms. Turn out onto a floured board and roll the dough out to about ¼ inch/5mm thick. Cut it into squares with a 2 inch/5cm biscuit cutter, gathering up and re-rolling until all the dough is used up. Transfer the squares to a greased baking sheet and bake in a preheated oven at 180°C/350°F/Gas mark 4 for about 15 minutes until golden. Carefully put the biscuits on a wire rack to cool.

Dried fruit savarin

> 8oz/225g mixed dried fruit (e.g. prune, fig, apple, pear, apricot, peach)
>
> 8oz/225g plain wholemeal flour
>
> 2oz/50g demerara sugar
>
> 2oz/50g vegan margarine, melted
>
> ½ sachet easy-blend yeast
>
> ½ teaspoon ground cinnamon
>
> 8 fl.oz/225ml soya milk, warmed
>
> 4 tablespoons prune juice
>
> apple and pear fruit spread

Put half of the dried fruit in a pan and cover with water. Bring to the boil, cover and simmer for about 15 minutes until soft. Drain and pat the fruit with kitchen paper to remove excess liquid, then cut it into even-sized chunks. Finely chop the remaining dried fruit and put it into a bowl with 2 table-spoonfuls of prune juice. Leave to soak for 45 minutes.

Put the flour, sugar, yeast and cinnamon in a bowl and mix in the soaked fruit and any remaining juice. Stir in the melted margarine and soya milk and combine thoroughly. Spoon the mixture into a greased 7 inch/18cm ring mould and level the top. Cover and leave in a warm place for 1 hour to rise. Bake in a preheated oven at 180°C/350°F/Gas mark 4 for about 25 minutes until browned. Run a sharp knife around the edges of the mould and turn the ring out onto a wire rack. Spoon the remaining prune juice evenly over the hot savarin and leave to cool. Spread the top with apple and pear fruit spread and arrange the chopped fruit on top before serving.

Nutty coffee, date and brandy cake

6oz/175g plain flour

2oz/50g vegan margarine

2oz/50g dried dates, finely chopped

2oz/50g mixed nuts, finely chopped

1½oz/40g demerara sugar

2 tablespoons brandy

1 tablespoon coffee powder or granules

1 rounded dessertspoon baking powder

6 fl.oz/175ml soya milk

filling

2oz/50g dried dates, chopped

4 fl.oz/125ml water

1oz/25g mixed nuts, grated

Soak the dates for the cake in the brandy for 30 minutes. Cream the margarine with the sugar and coffee in a large bowl, add the soaked dates and any remaining brandy and mix well. Keep 2 tablespoonfuls of chopped nuts and add the rest to the bowl. Add the sifted flour and baking powder alternately with the soya milk, combining well between additions. Spoon the mixture into a lined and greased 7 inch/18cm round cake tin and level the top. Sprinkle the remaining chopped nuts on top and press these in lightly with the back of a spoon. Cover loosely with foil and bake in a preheated oven at 180°C/350°F/Gas mark 4 for 20 minutes. Remove the foil and bake for another 10 minutes or so until firm in the centre. Carefully transfer to a wire rack to cool.

Put the dates for the filling and the water in a small pan and bring to the boil. Simmer, while stirring occasionally to break up the dates, until the liquid has been absorbed and the mixture is thick. Remove from the heat, stir in the grated nuts and allow to cool.

Using a sharp long knife, carefully cut the cake through the middle to make 2 circles. Spread the filling evenly on the bottom layer and replace the top. Cut into wedges to serve.

Fruited couronne

12oz/350g plain flour

½ sachet easy-blend yeast

½ teaspoon salt

1oz/25g vegan margarine, melted

approx. 6 fl.oz/175ml soya milk, warmed

4oz/100g dried apricots, finely chopped

4 fl.oz/125ml fresh apple juice

2oz/50g glacé cherries, washed, dried and chopped

2oz/50g raisins, chopped

1oz/25g walnuts, finely chopped

1 tablespoon sugar-free apricot jam

1 dessertspoon water

Mix the flour, yeast and salt, add the melted margarine and combine well. Gradually add the soya milk until a soft dough forms. Knead the dough thoroughly, then return it to the bowl and leave in a warm place for 35 minutes to rise.

Put the apricots and apple juice in a small saucepan and bring to the boil. Cover and simmer gently until the liquid has been absorbed, then remove from the heat and mash the apricots with the back of a spoon.

Turn the dough out onto a floured board and knead again. Roll it out into an oblong measuring 14 x 9 inches/35 x 23cm. Spread the apricots evenly over the dough and scatter the cherries, raisins and walnuts over the apricots. Roll the dough up tightly like a Swiss roll, then squeeze or roll it so that it lengthens to about 20 inches/51cm. Cut the roll in half lengthwise and twist the two halves together, keeping the cut sides uppermost. Form this twist into a ring shape on a greased baking sheet and press the edges together to join. Cover and leave to rise in a warm place for an hour. Bake in a preheated oven at 200°C/400°F/Gas mark 6 for about 15 minutes until golden brown. Heat the apricot jam with the water in a small pan until runny. Brush the glaze over the ring and let it cool slightly before cutting into slices.

Alsace prune and walnut cake (serves 8)

6oz/175g fine wholemeal self raising flour

2oz/50g vegan margarine

2oz/50g demerara sugar

¼ teaspoon ground cinnamon

6 fl.oz/175ml soya milk

topping

6oz/175g prunes, stoned and chopped

1oz/25g walnuts, chopped

5 fl.oz/150ml fresh apple juice

Soak the prunes in the apple juice for 2 hours, then bring to the boil. Cover and simmer for about 10 minutes until the juice has been absorbed. Remove from the heat and stir in the walnuts. Sift the flour and cinnamon into a mixing bowl, rub in the margarine, then stir in the sugar. Gradually add the soya milk and mix thoroughly. Spoon the mixture into a lined and greased 7 inch/18cm square baking tin. Spread it out evenly, then spoon the prune and walnut mixture on top, pressing it in lightly with the back of a spoon, Bake in a preheated oven at 180°C/350°F/Gas mark 4 for 25 minutes. Carefully turn out onto a wire rack to cool before cutting into slices.